TRACES OF THE PAST

The fiftieth anniversary publication of the new Beth Yehuda
Synagogue chronicles a rich and detailed history of the congregation.

Traces of the Past

Montreal's Early Synagogues

Sara Ferdman Tauben

WITH A PORTFOLIO OF PHOTOGRAPHS BY
DAVID KAUFMAN

Véhicule Press

Published with the generous assistance of The Canada Council for the Arts, the Book Publishing Industry Development Program of the Department of Canadian Heritage and the Société de développement des entreprises culturelles du Québec (SODEC).

Cover design: J.W. Stewart
Front cover photograph: David Kaufman
Maps by Dave Goulet
Set in Adobe Minion by Simon Garamond
Printed by Marquis Book Printing Inc.

LIBRARY AND ARCHIVES CANADA CATALOGUING IN PUBLICATION

Tauben, Sara Ferdman
Traces of the past : Montreal's early synagogues / Sara Ferdman Tauben ; with a portfolio of photographs by David Kaufman.

Includes index.
ISBN 978-1-55065-316-8

1. Synagogues–Québec (Province)–Montréal–History.
2. Jews–Québec (Province)–Montréal–History. I. Kaufman, David, 1948. II. Title.

FC2947.9.J4T38 2011   296.6'50971428   C2011-901221-9

Published by Véhicule Press, Montréal, Québec, Canada
www.vehiculepress.com

Distribution in Canada by LitDistCo
www.litdistco.ca

Distribution in U.S. by Independent Publishers Group
www.ipgbook.com

Printed in Canada on 100% post-consumer recycled paper.

To my husband, Irwin Tauben,
who makes everything possible;

to the city that adopted me and
the community that embraced me.

Contents

Preface

"Our old Orthodox synagogues [are] monuments of our past that are now disappearing …. The traces of the role that these orthodox synagogues played in local Jewish life must not disappear."[1]

—B.G. Sack

IN 1958, WHEN HISTORIAN B.G. Sack wrote an article documenting the old synagogues of Montreal, the congregations were already moving to post-war suburbs. By 1999, when I began my hunt, there was scant physical evidence. Traces of former synagogues dot the urban landscape of the neighbourhoods they once inhabited as Jewish houses of worship. Their previous function is revealed by markings chiselled away by weather, time, and subsequent inhabitants. Here and there, the name of a congregation, a Hebrew inscription, or a glimpse of a Star of David can still be detected beneath scratch marks, or partially concealed by layers of renovations. In the rear of many buildings that once housed synagogues, circular tracings in the brick silently recall the stained-glass windows that once illuminated the space above the Ark of the Torah.

Nevertheless, as in any detective story, a series of assumptions and truths can be derived from disparate pieces of evidence. Historic city maps and directories, sepia-coloured photos, brittle newspaper articles, long-forgotten anniversary publications, even something as incidental as announcements of meetings, served as clues. Additionally, the expertise of specialists and testimony of eyewitnesses lent invaluable assistance in understanding and interpreting these traces of the past.

I am indebted to the Centre for Jewish Art at Hebrew University and to the late Professor Betzalel Narkiss, the founder and initiating director, for having inspired and encouraged this study in the first place. The Centre for Jewish Art is dedicated to documenting Jewish art and material culture around the world.

Originally written as a master's thesis in Judaic Studies at Concordia University, my work has benefited from the interest, encouragement, and participation of more people than I ever imagined it might when I embarked upon my journey through the archives and streets of Montreal in search of its early synagogues.

Professor Ira Robinson, my thesis advisor, lent the benefit of his prodigious knowledge, wise guidance, and constant encouragement throughout a process that became much longer than either of us expected. Professor Richard Menkis, a visiting professor from the University of British Columbia, pointed out an analytical direction that proved to be a turning point in my investigation.

Professor Peter Jacobs introduced me to his colleague Susan Bronson, from the masters program in the conservation of the built environment in the School of Architecture of the Université de Montréal, initiating an invaluable working relationship and fulfilling friendship. Professor Bronson supervised graduate students Isabelle Bouchard and Gabriel Malo in a summer project documenting all buildings which served as synagogues in the Plateau Mont-Royal over the course of the twentieth century. The resulting inventory addressed and responded to most of the questions I could not have answered on my own. Additionally, I gained some insights into the knowledge base and methods of the field of heritage architecture. Most significantly, as they confirmed that the majority of synagogues were housed in former residences, I became convinced that my story would encompass not only buildings of architectural significance but also those of humble or little architectural value.

I am also grateful to the Jewish Public Library and the Mile End Library for mounting the students' exhibits and hosting our joint programs. We were also extraordinarily fortunate to have benefited from the artistic eye of photographer David Kaufman, who volunteered his time and skills to photograph many of the buildings in the summer of 2000.

Of course, this book would not have materialized without my editor and publisher, Simon Dardick, who also contributed points of interest to the walking tours based on his own knowledge of the neighbourhood he calls home.

I wish to acknowledge the professionalism and assistance of head archivist Janice Rosen of Canadian Jewish Congress Archives as well as the help of Eiren Harris, volunteer archivist at the Jewish Public Library.

As well, I thank my daughter, Evelyn Tauben, for compiling a bibliography on synagogue architecture, and my mother, Rochelle Ferdman, who helped me in reading and translating the hand-written minute book of the Anshei Ozeroff.

I am particularly grateful for those who were willing to share their memories and mementos as former residents of Montreal's old Jewish neighbourhoods: Isadore Albin, Morty Bercovitch, Harvey Berger, Rachel Birnbaum, Sylvia Chernoff Bolten, Sylvia Reuven Brasloff, Olive Golick Brumer, Edward Caplansky, Yoel Colton, Helen Parnass Constantine, Arch Crystal, Ben Zion Dalphen, Ron Finegold, Ann Tannenbaum Goodman Gold, Hilda Silberman Golick, Rena Steinberg Gornitsky, Judge Irving Halperin, Sara Solomon Jacobs, Bracha Kaplan, Philip Madres, Sylvia Salzman Madres, Fay Colton Magid, Yolette (Lola) Vool Mendelson, Ruth Wotkov Pinsky, Lawrence Popliger, Stanley Rappoport, Joseph Rapaport, Allan Raymond, Chava Kaplan Respitz, Louis Sheiner, Simon Sperber, Harry Stillman, Bill Surkis, Isaac Tennenbaum, Rose Tennenbaum-Zuckerman, Nan Wiseman, Jack Zuckerman, Judy Zuckerman Cohen, Allan Tennenbaum, Edward Wolkove, Gertrude Bolten Yanofsky, Shulamis Borodensky Yelin, Jean Birenbaum Zwirek. Their stories revealed information about the immigrant experience and their personal relationship to the synagogues, in particular, that would not otherwise have been available.

Finally, the story that has emerged describes the synagogues and their congregations, and is, therefore, a story of buildings and of the Jewish community which inhabited them and invested them with meaning.

Introduction

> At that time a great windstorm swept over the world....Since
> the wind came and turned the entire world around...the old
> paths are no longer of any use. We are now in need of new
> paths, because all the places have been altered. We do, however,
> retain an imprint of those times and that in itself is very great.
>
> —Rabbi Nachman of Bratislav, 1810[1]

THE DECADES SURROUNDING the turn of the twentieth-century
marked the era of mass migration of the Jews of Eastern Europe.
Fleeing poverty and persecution, the largest numbers made their
way from Russia to the United States, joining other groups of
immigrants in forming the most densely populated neighbourhoods in the world on New York's Lower East Side.[2] Many came
to Montreal. Leaving places with names like Minsk, Pinsk, Morosh,
Galicia, and Dinovitz, they settled on streets with names like St.
Urbain, St. Dominique and St. Laurent. So as to retain familiar
traditions and familial connections, they established small congregations which recalled the homes they left behind. The Pinsker
Shul, Anshei Morosh, Anshei Ukraina, and Anshei Ozeroff were
not only places of worship but also places where friends and family,
landsleit from the same country, area, or town could meet, exchange
concerns, lend support to each other and resolve to help those left
behind. This is a story that attempts to describe and define social,
religious, economic, and existential aspects of a distinct group of
people through the remnants of its material culture. Similar to an
archeological study, the physical remains of the past were first
located, identified, and described and then their meaning and

function were interpreted within the context of a particular cultural setting and historic time. The movement and development of the Jewish community of Montreal from the 1880s until 1945 has been tracked by mapping the location of synagogues. Some understanding can be gained of the process of adaptation of the immigrant community by interpreting the buildings as reflections of the congregations' identities and as a measure of their aspirations.

The study of material culture focuses not only on the monumental and extraordinary, but especially on the mundane and ordinary. The study of Jewish material culture poses particular challenges and confronts certain preconceptions. Judaism is associated with word, Christianity with image. It may be assumed that Jewish art, due to biblical injunction, does not even exist and that any Jewish material products are irrelevant in defining "authentic" Jewish culture as they are merely copies of that produced by Gentile culture. This conception is derived from the Second Commandment:

> You shall not make for yourself a sculptured image, or any likeness of what is in the heavens above or on the earth below, or in the waters below the earth. You shall not bow down to them or serve them...(Exodus 20.4-5)

However, the Bible recounts that the house of God itself, Solomon's Temple, contained sculpted images of cherubim, oxen, and lions. In the same chapter in which the Second Commandment is pronounced, the artistry of Bezalel is extolled:

> [He is] endowed...with a divine spirit of skill, ability, and knowledge in every kind of craft: to make designs for work in gold, silver, and copper, to cut stones, for setting and to carve wood—to work in every kind of craft. (Exodus 31.3-5)

Not only Judaism, but Christianity and Islam as well, had to contend with the implications of the Second Commandment.

Joseph Gutmann's *No Graven Images* examines attitudes to figurative imagery in the Bible and throughout various historic periods and concludes that "no uniform, unchanging attitude toward images has prevailed within Jewish history—or for that matter, within Christian or Muslim societies."[3]

The scholastic understanding of the role of imagery, art, aesthetics, and material culture in general should constitute an ongoing concern of academic curiosity in cultures that have inherited these traditions. Yet, notwithstanding the prodigious contribution of Christianity to the pictorial and architectural heritage of Western culture, scholars of both architectural and art history find a need to assert their role in the task of writing history and defining cultures, claiming that the investigation of the built environment and of aesthetics is as valid an endeavour as the study of the record of ideas and intellectual discourse embedded in texts.

In the preface to a collection of essays entitled *Cultures of the Jews,* editor David Biale describes a small fifteenth-century silver box, a wedding gift within which the new Jewish homemaker could store the keys to her linen chest. It includes a series of dials, labelled in Hebrew numbers that serve to keep track of the pieces of linen in the household storage. Surprisingly perhaps, in the context of a presumably traditional community, it features both clothed and nude women. This poses questions about the Jewish culture of the time which might not appear in, or might even be contradicted by, textual evidence. Was there a different standard of acceptability for private versus public expression? Were Jewish sensibilities influenced by the aesthetics of the Italian Renaissance culture? Biale proposes that "culture is the practice of everyday life. It is what people do, what they say about what they do, and finally, how they understand both of these activities. If Jewish culture is broadly conceived along these lines, objects like the silver casket are as precious repositories of meaning as learned texts."[4]

Architectural historian John Gloag, has written a history of Western civilization by tracing the development of the built environment from antiquity to modern times, describing not only monumental public structures serving kings, priests, and aristocracy but the humble abodes of slaves, peasants, and labourers. Throughout Gloag asserts "the interpretive quality of architecture." "Buildings can not lie," he wrote, "they tell the truth directly or by implication about those who made and used them and provide veracious records of the character and quality of past and present civilizations.... Irrespective of time or place, the interpretative quality in architecture persists..."[5]

Similarly, Richard I. Cohen in *Jewish Icons: Art and Society in Modern Europe* claims that all material artifacts are potentially informative. Referring to himself as a social historian, Cohen articulates his position: "Open to all types of visual material and without differentiating between high and low culture, I am convinced that visual arts talk history and constitute history."[6] Not only that which may be defined as art, but also the "stuff" of daily life, "clothes, food, furniture, souvenirs, knickknacks, photographs, monuments, [as well as] established masterpieces become part of the historian's terrain."[7]

Cohen's work focuses on the material world created by European Jewry confronting modernity. The category of "portraiture of Jews" serves as an interesting example, debunking the myth that Jews, even the most traditional, did not portray the human image. In exploring the theme of "Rabbi as Icon,"[8] Cohen describes the proliferation of rabbinic portraiture during the late eighteenth and nineteenth centuries. In the context of the challenge of modernizing trends and reform, rabbinic portraiture became an important means of signifying status and reinforcing rabbinic authority. With apparently little hesitation on the part of the rabbis, and aided by new production technologies, portraits of rabbis became cherished household objects as "icons" of authority and "amulets" of protective power, transforming the rabbis into "folk heroes." Often crafted by women or within the woman's household realm, rabbinic images appeared on such mundane objects as embroidery and dishware. That the rabbis themselves were often not only conscious of but also solicitous of the opportunity of popularizing their images is evidenced by a portrait of Rabbi Zevi Hirsch Chajes illustrating his commentary on the Talmud published in 1843. Rabbi Chajes wrote the inscription on his own portrait: "Now he will be joyful and happy and find pleasure/That his picture will be seen for his face shines light."[9]

Possibly no one understood and expressed the process of concretization of persons and things into icons better than twentieth-century artist Andy Warhol. In the rapidly expanding market of mass production and mass media of the sixties, the extraordinary and the ordinary became equally visible. The face of Marilyn Monroe was no more or less prominent than the image of a Campbell's soup can label and both were equally attainable at your local newstand or supermarket. Jackie Kennedy, an icon of grace and culture, was as present in our world, her face reprinted in multiple monochromatic images, as stacks of boxes of Brillo soap pads. In an exhibit at the Montreal Museum of Fine Arts, Warhol's oversized soap pad boxes are installed next to a Lucite tower encasing and entitled "Warhol's Garbage."[10] This tower, by Armand Pierre Fernandez, pays homage to Warhol's appreciation of material culture. During the cleaning of Warhol's residence following his death, boxes of refuse, though not garbage, were found in storage. Magazines, newspapers, playbills, invitations, letters, event tickets, etc. were casually tossed into boxes creating a chronological strata of things representing Warhol's daily life, the everyday world which he inhabited, perhaps not as ordinary, but yet not so different from others who shared it.

It is from this sort of "stuff" that a measure of understanding emerges regarding an immigrant community, providing a glimpse into its aspirations and adaptations to a new environment, and clues as to what may have been transmitted in passage and transformed in a new place.

Areas of Settlement

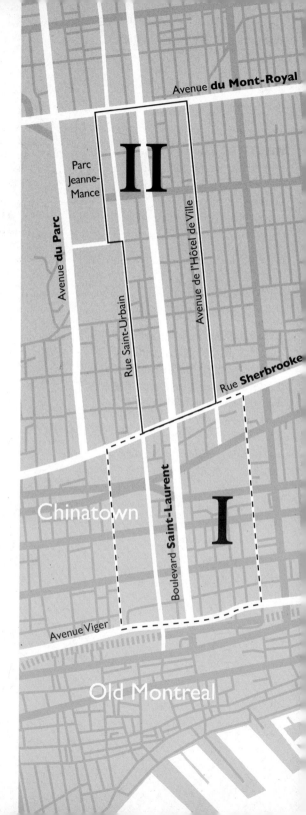

Area II is bordered by avenue du Mont-Royal on the north, rue Sherbrooke on the south, avenue de l'Hôtel de Ville on the east and parc Jeanne-Mance, otherwise known as Fletcher's Field, on the west.

Area I, the early enclave, is bordered by rue Sherbrooke on the north and the river on the south, the synagogues being above avenue Viger. The east-west boundaries are less clear but appear to be just east and west of boulevard Saint-Laurent.

AREAS OF SETTLEMENT

Area IV is bordered by rue Hutchison on the east, and then encompasses Outremont in general.

Area III is bordered by avenue du Mont-Royal on the south, avenue Bernard on the north, boulevard Saint-Laurent on the east and rue Hutchison on the west.

[CHAPTER ONE]

Harbingers of Great Institutions

The corner of St. Urbain and Dorchester was the very heart of
the Jewish neighbourhood. Nearby was Dufferin Park, then a
"Jewish Park" where Jewish immigrants went to breathe the
fresh air, meet their *landslayt*, hear the latest news, look for
work and read the newspapers.

Continuing our walk, we approach Craig Street where all the
side streets and lanes such as St. Urbain, Clark (then St. Charles-
Borromée), St. George, Coté, Hermine, St. Dominque, and
Cadieux [now De Bullion], were inhabited exclusively by Jews.[11]
–Israel Medres

ISRAEL MEDRES IMMIGRATED to Montreal from Russia in 1910
and became a well-known journalist for the Yiddish daily, the
Keneder Adler. He invites us to "take a stroll through Montreal of
yesterday" visiting the old Jewish neighbourhoods. When the early
Eastern European immigrants began arriving in Montreal in the
1880s they found a small Jewish community of about 800[12], largely
concentrated in an area of several blocks known today as Old
Montreal and Chinatown. Socially and economically well-established,
the community already had an institutional base of several
philanthropic societies and three synagogues. The Shearith Israel,
or the Spanish and Portuguese congregation, the first Jewish congregation established in Canada in 1768, built its second synagogue
in 1838 at the corner of Dufferin Park on Chenneville. Only blocks
away, the Corporation of English, German and Polish Jews built
their first synagogue in 1859. This Ashkenazi congregation, later
known as the Shaar Hashomayim, had been formed by former
members of the Shearith Israel in 1846. Liberal-minded members
of the Ashkenazi congregation, under the influence of their rabbi,

(Top) The Shearith Israel built its second synagogue in 1838
on Chenneville Street.
(Bottom) Temple Emanu-El, founded in 1882, Montreal's first
Reform congregation, was built iin 1892.

who "was imbued with the current enlightenment," broke away to establish Montreal's first Reform congregation in 1882 following a conflict over women's participation in the Simchat Torah celebration.[13] Initially renting premises in a hall and later constructing their own synagogue, Temple Emanu-El was the first congregation outside the early enclave.[14] In the eighties and nineties the Shearith Israel and Shaar Hashomayim re-established themselves "uptown," following their congregants whose economic and social standing allowed them to move to Montreal's "Golden Mile," today's downtown or *centreville*. This westward move, while representing a migration of not more than a kilometre, marked the beginning of a divide that was to characterize the community until after World War II. Though representing differing liturgical practices and orientations, these three congregations had much in common socially and economically, and were viewed by the increasing numbers of immigrants filling the downtown neighbourhoods as the rich "uptowners." This "uptown-downtown" dichotomy also represented a significant ideological and cultural division. While the guttural sounds and singsong intonations of Yiddish filled the streets, shops, and *shuln* of the downtown neighbourhoods, English was the language of daily life in the businesses, social clubs, country clubs,[15] and synagogue meeting rooms of the "uptowners." To highlight the contrast between the uptown and downtown congregations and their synagogues, a brief analysis of the uptown congregations will serve as a counterpoint before pursuing our primary interest, the "downtowners."

The "Uptowners"

The Shearith Israel marked its 150th anniversary in 1918 with a publication honouring its history and its illustrious founding members, "men who by their energy and initiative were helping, even in those early days, to lay the foundations of Canada's future greatness."[16] Names of the seventeenth and eighteenth centuries like Hart, Joseph, David, Solomon, Frank, Levy, Samuels, and Hays were prominent not only in the Jewish community but also in the economic and political development of the city. Special tribute was paid to Abraham de Sola, the spiritual leader of the congregation from 1847-1882, who ranked "among the foremost Jewish savants of his day and acquired a reputation that was well-nigh world-wide..."[17]

De Sola was a highly regarded and well known intellectual in the English as well as the Jewish community. He joined the faculty of McGill College and was a member of various Anglophone intellectual societies. Abraham de Sola's sons succeeded him as foremost leaders of the Jewish community. Meldola de Sola served as spiritual leader of the Shearith Israel after his father's death. Clarence de Sola was credited as a leading force behind the building of the new synagogue in 1890 where he served as *parnas* for many years. He filled a historic role as first president of the Canadian Zionist Federation from 1898 until shortly before his death in 1919.

Such a distinguished history deserved a fitting architectural statement, one that was both Jewish and cosmopolitan. The building which they had left behind on Chenneville was a small neo-classical structure with nothing to distinguish it as a synagogue. But the neo-classical façade of the new synagogue, built in 1890 on Stanley Street, expressed oriental features, a reference to Judaism's eastern origins. The framework and proportions of the window and doors, and particularly the lotus flower columns, evoke Egyptian architecture. This same feature appeared in the interior decorating the capitals of the columns supporting the women's gallery and the carved wood detailing on the *aron hakodesh*. The building is described as being in the "Judeo-Egyptian style.... The architecture and ornamentation throughout are pervaded by Jewish characteristics, every detail being studied to that effect."[18]

The adoption of these styles was a direct transference of the architecture of nineteenth-century European synagogues built in appreciation or in anticipation of political emancipation, the granting

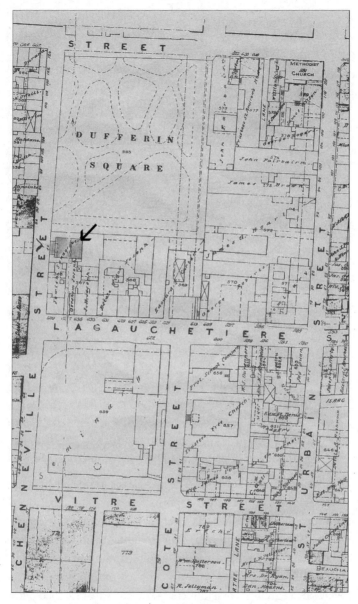

In 1838 Shearith Israel (*see arrow*) built their synagogue in what is
now Chinatown. The entire block is now occupied
by an office complex.

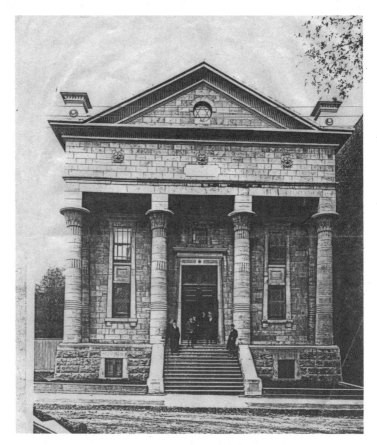

The Shearith Israel Synagogue was built on Stanley Street in 1890. The lotus flower columns evoked Egyptian architecture.

of citizenship and equal rights. The neo-classical and neo-Egyptian styles originated in the early period of the emancipation of European Jewry. The neo-classical revival in architecture generally is associated with the era of the Enlightenment with its ideals of rational philosophy, scientific inquiry, and humanistic values which found artistic expression in the art of antiquity and the Renaissance. Architectural influences also arose from archeological discoveries of the nineteenth century, including ancient synagogues. Egyptian influences appeared in architecture following Napoleon's expedition of 1798 and remained popular in Europe and America until the middle of the nineteenth century. Despite the negative reminder of the enslavement of the Jews, architectural references to Egypt were incorporated in synagogue architecture as indicative of strength and longevity, both historically and architecturally. For the Jews of Europe this style served as an expression of support for Napoleon and the ideals of the French Revolution.[19] The reference to the architectural styles of antiquity was also expressed in the neo-Roman synagogue of the Shearith Israel of New York built in 1897 which continued the use of classical styles expressed in the congregation's two earlier buildings.[20] Like its Montreal namesake, the New York congregation followed the Spanish and Portuguese tradition and was the first synagogue in the United States, established in 1654. In many respects, the building resembles the Shearith Israel of Montreal but unlike the Montreal building, whose distinctive lotus columns provided a Judaic reference, and despite the architect's intention to reflect the synagogues of ancient Galilee, New York's Shearith Israel was indistinguishable from any neo-classical American bank or federal building. Perhaps we can conclude that it was with a certain sense of self-confidence that the Montreal congregation chose to articulate its ethnicity on the façade of its synagogue.

During the course of the nineteenth century, the ideals of nationalism and Romanticism began to replace the ideals of the Enlightenment in Europe. The aspirations of developing nation-states fostered the writing of national histories and the creation of national myths and aesthetics. In architecture these aspirations led to the revival of a multitude of historic styles. In the search for appropriate styles for synagogue architecture, a debate arose considering two conceptual options: one that served to distinguish the particularity of the Jewish nation and the other linking the Jews with the architectural heritage of European nations.

In Lodz, Poland, the Orthodox and Reform congregations purposely selected contrasting styles. A Polish architectural historian

New York's Shearith Israel was built in 1897. Although similar to Montreal's Shearith Israel, it was indistinguishable from many neo-classical American banks or federal buildings.

interpreted the meaning of this architectural dialogue as follows: "Through the colourful Moresque architectural clothing the indigenous Orthodox Jews emphasized their attachment to a religious and cultural tradition whose roots lie in the Near East, opposing the assimilative tendencies of the progressive Jews" of the Reform Synagogue who chose the Romanesque style, which was seen as linked to French and German origin.[21] The Moorish style is often typified by surface ornamentation, as in the dark and light banding of the Lodz synagogue, and in distinctive fenestration. The Romanesque style is most particularly characterized by round arches. Neo-Romanesque borrows as well from the Renaissance, as with the multiple domes of the Lodz synagogue.

The participants in the debate of an appropriate synagogue style were both Christian and Jewish architects (who had begun to enter the profession by the mid-century), governmental

Synagogues of Lodz
(Top) Moorish-Orthodox, 1865.
(Bottom) Neo-Romanesque-Reform, *circa* 1881.

authorities, and Jewish lay and religious leaders.[22] During the design process for a synagogue in Kassel, Germany, the Egyptian design proposed by the local government was rejected by the Jewish community in favour of a style combining classic and Romanesque elements. The architects selected by the community, August Schuchardt and his Jewish associate, A. Rosengarten, argued that the Egyptian style was foreign to both Germany and Judaism. This design, and the arguments supporting it published by Rosengarten, proved to be particularly influential, and out of the fray of the battle for appropriate synagogue styles, the Romanesque emerged as the most prominent.[23]

The first building erected by the Reform congregation Temple Emanu-El in 1892 was a small structure whose design features defy stylistic classification (p. 22). While the arched windows and doorway reflect the Romanesque influence, it is the prominent Star of David stained-glass window which confidently marked the building as a synagogue in the burgeoning centre of the city. The congregation's

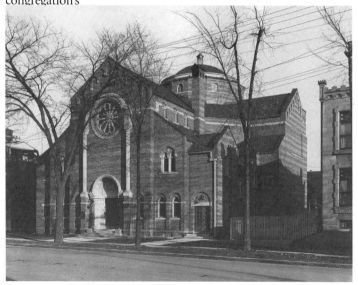

Temple Emanu-El on Sherbrooke Street, Westmount, 1911.

building of 1911, in its present location in the affluent municipality of Westmount, was, however, well-articulated and may have been among the city's first examples of the Romanesque-Byzantine style.[24] In 1932 Temple Emanu-El marked its fiftieth anniversary. The texts of its anniversary publication stress particularly its stalwart role as the initiator and leader of Reform Judaism in Canada, its history a "graphic tale of the opposition it had been forced to encounter in a city so thoroughly conservative as Montreal."[25]

A poem, though printed in a 1970 publication, nevertheless, speaks eloquently to the choice of a rather sturdy and even stern Byzantine style.

> Yours no lofty spires, pointing as they rise
> With a slender finger toward the vaulted skies…
> Cupped toward earth, your structure naught of awe commands,
> Only quiet sanctuary as it stands…
> Yours no overbearing, intricate design,
> Only simple beauty in each graceful line…[26]

The architecture is a metaphor for a religious philosophy that unpretentiously asserts its position among more commanding ideologies. The reference to "lofty spires" and "intricate design" might be deriding the excesses of Gothic churches or the minarets and Moorish lacey ornamentation of late nineteenth early twentieth-century synagogues such as the McGill College location of the Shaar Hashomayim.

In this era of historic revivalism the terms Romanesque and Byzantine were often used synonymously, the central dome, as that of Temple Emanu-El, being the feature which most clearly distinguished the Byzantine. Moorish elements were often mixed with Romanesque or Byzantine, the minarets or onion domes perhaps being the most interesting feature. German architect Ludwig Forester began a trend when he designed synagogues in Vienna and Budapest featuring prominent twin minarets. These, he asserted, evoked the twin columns, Joachim and Boaz, of Solomon's Temple. The soaring minarets of the Shaar Hashomayim, built in 1886, the

Dohany Street Synagogue, Budapest, 1854-59.

prominent central window with intricate grill work, and the peaked pediment, formed a clear expression of the Moorish style.[27]

But then and even today, the most prominent congregation and impressive synagogue was the Shaar Hashomayim on Kensington Avenue in Westmount. Both the stature of its constituency and its edifice were honoured at the time of the dedication of the building in 1922. The synagogue recognized among its members those who had demonstrated significant leadership in the communal affairs of the city of Montreal and the Dominion of Canada.

> This new Synagogue is an achievement which they [the founders] could hardly have thought possible .... A structure, cathedral-like in its imposing proportions, and dominating its immediate surroundings, it breathes the very life of stateliness and permanence. Built in a grey vitrified brick and sandstone, it is capped by a series of small Moorish cupolas that lend a touch of mystic orientalism to the whole...[28]

Contrary to the above description, there are no distinctive Moorish features in the 1922 building. It is, instead, a fine example of Romano-Byzantine synagogue architecture. The round arches, portals, and dome exemplify the German *Rundbogenstil* style of the round arches. It is, nevertheless, instructive that the chronicler

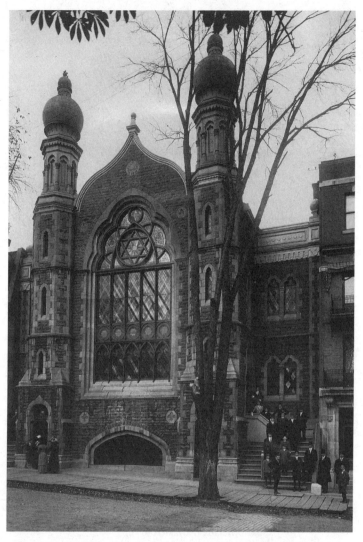

The Shaar Hashomayim, with its soaring minarets on McGill Avenue,
was built in 1886.

(Top and bottom)The Shaar Hashomayin on Kensington Avenue was officially dedicated in 1922.

perceived this building as being particularly Moorish and connected to "orientalism." The Romanesque round arch does originally derive from the orient and it is this feature which came to most prominently distinguish Montreal's early synagogues from the Gothic churches of the city.

Important "modern" elements were introduced to the interior layout. These features were influenced by the Reform movement and were already evident in Orthodox synagogues in Europe, particularly in countries of Germanic influence. The traditional separate *bimah* facing the Ark was replaced by a reading table facing the congregation on a stage in front of the Ark. The women's sec-tion also received a new placement: "Two loges raised about two feet from the floor, flanking the sides are reserved for the ladies, and replace the old fashioned galleries."[29]

With their words, these "uptown" congregations expressed a sense of their historic and present significance not only within Montreal Jewry but also Canadian Jewry and even Canadian social and economic development. Not only did their buildings reflect this deserved stature in their monumentality, but they were also representative of the European and North American search for an architectural synagogue style and vocabulary in the late nineteenth and early twentieth centuries.

The Early Downtowners

During the 1890s and the first two decades of the twentieth century, a steady stream of immigration increased the Jewish population of Montreal in 1901 to almost 8,000 and in 1911 to nearly 29,000.[30] The downtown immigrant community maintained its own momentum of institution building, establishing philanthropic, benevolent, social and educational institutions, some of which provided the foundations of future organizations. Many of the early immigrant synagogues were also harbingers of great institutions. Most of the approximately one dozen Eastern European congregations which had established themselves by the end of the first decade within the first area of settlement were probably small *minyans* worshipping in rented commercial lofts or houses. But a few exhibited aspirations for buildings which matched their collective sense of communal leadership.

The fiftieth anniversary booklet of the Beth Yehuda in 1940 suggests that the congregation recognized its date of origin as being around 1890 when a small congregation of Hasidim established Ohel Moshe in honor of their *rebbe's* son. Worshipping initially in the home of a rabbi, they subsequently rented space in larger homes as the congregation grew. After some time, financial constraints notwithstanding, some members began to advocate in favour of acquiring their own building. Purchasing a former theatre which was renovated into "quite a fine *shul*," the congregation chose a new name, Beth Yehuda. The new building attracted new members, reducing its financial difficulties. As the chronicler concludes, the Beth Yehuda became well-known within the entire Jewish community as one of the most beautiful synagogues of Montreal.[31]

The first synagogue built by the new immigrant community was the Chevra Kadisha. As its name indicates, it was originally established in 1893 as a benevolent burial society providing ritual burial services to members of the Jewish community regardless of their financial means. The society maintained this service until 1912 when Lazarus Paperman established Montreal's first Jewish commercial burial service. The congregation's original constitution indicates as well that the burial society would maintain its own place of worship. One can assume that despite its benevolent function, the society must have had a fair number of paying customers, for within ten years it had erected one of Montreal's largest synagogues at the time. Indeed, a newspaper article of 1899 reported that "The financial condition of the society is flourishing, they having been able to purchase a hearse for exclusive Jewish use, and to completely pay off the cost of a Jewish cemetery at Sault-au-Récollet..."[32] An article reporting on the cornerstone-

The Chevra Kadisha Synagogue on St. Urbain Street.

laying on August 1, 1902 provides an indication of the condition of the current premises, while describing the plans for the new building:

> The present synagogue of the congregation is in the tumble-down houses of the lower part of St. Urbain Street. Apparently two of them have been knocked down into one, and the upper floor of one of them has been retained as a gallery for the women.
>
> The new synagogue will be a handsome structure, with a cut stone front, of Hebraic design. It will have two large towers, with Eastern cupolas at the summit and a large doorway in the centre, with a flight of steps leading up to it.... [It] will seat nearly 800 people, while the basement will be given up to classrooms.[33]

The dominant feature of the building, the two "Eastern cupolas," was a common element of synagogue architecture of this era in Europe and America. The reporter, whether Jewish or not, recognizes this as being "of Hebraic design." There were no other markings, except for perhaps the name of the congregation, indicating that the building was a synagogue, and yet its function was obvious. The building was large and located on a prominent street. Certainly it was intended as a statement of confidence and permanence. Unfortunately, it was destroyed by fire in 1920.

Though smaller in stature, the B'nai Jacob Synagogue may have exceeded the Chevra Kadisha in communal importance. The congregation acquired the former Shaar Hashomayim Synagogue in 1886. Originally named the Sons of Benjamin, the congregation took on the name B'nai Jacob in honour of a major benefactor, Jacob Gelber, at the time of the renovation. As we shall see, this was a rather common practice. Synagogue names that appear to refer to Biblical figures were more likely those of a prominent patron, providing nevertheless, a double honour; recognizing the significant contribution while linking the benefactor to an important religious personage. The original synagogue was either demolished or, more likely, renovated and extended to provide for a larger capacity of five hundred. The renovations were carried out by the same architect who had designed the Chevra Kadisha, Eric Mann. A newspaper article of 1899 alludes to the congregation's success and prominence, largely attributed to the leadership of Rabbi A.M. Ashinsky. "Indeed so great is the influence of Rabbi Ashinsky that every Saturday afternoon the synagogue is crowded by Jews of all classes who come eagerly to listen to his interesting sermons.... The financial state of the congregation is [as well] in a flourishing condition, they having paid for their synagogue and for a plot in the Jewish cemetery of Back River."[34]

In taking over the building of the former Shaar Hashomayim, the B'nai Jacob seems to have also taken over its communal role within the neighbourhood. "Between her walls," B.G. Sack wrote, "the most important Jewish gatherings in Montreal used to take place." In 1896 Rabbi Ashinsky founded the city's first Talmud Torah and a year later helped to establish the Canadian Zionist organization, all "between these walls." Sack remarked that not only did the B'nai Jacob serve as a place of assembly for these formal meetings "where Jewish leaders, the founders and builders of that time, would gather to discuss the matters and subjects that were important to the community," but also that "Jews of all kinds used to come not only to worship, but to socialize, simply to chat [*chap a shmooze*]."[35]

The original constitution of the B'nai Jacob of 1886 is still extant. It is a proper and formal constitution following the content and structure of bylaws of any formally constituted organization. It outlines the roles and responsibilities of the officers as well as the traditional synagogue officials, the *parnas*, *shammash*, and *gabbai*. It stipulates the conditions and benefits of membership. Expected conduct and attendance of members and officers in the *shul* and at meetings are clearly indicated as are fines for transgressions. Ultimate authority clearly resides in the president, sometimes in consultation with the *parnas*, a position often melded with that of president in other congregations. But the general principle of behaviour is expressed in the article entitled "Achdut," unity or solidarity. "Every member is responsible for respecting the other. Every member is responsible for seeing that in the association there is peace and not division."

The language of the constitution bears comment. Despite the fact that Article 2 stipulates that "the language of business will be English," the constitution is written in Yiddish. The Yiddish is, however, heavily anglicized. The document contains not only individual English words inherent in organizational vocabulary, such as regular, special, and general meeting, but utilizes English verbs conjugated into Yiddish such as *attendn* or *instructn*, and idiomatic expressions translated directly into Yiddish, such as "call to order." This would be surprising for such an early document representing a congregation of recent immigrants. The nature of the Yiddish strengthens an assumption of historian Bernard Figler "that among the founders of B'nai Jacob Congregation of Russian and Polish Jews were former members of the older Congregation of English, German, and Polish [the Shaar Hashomayim]. [Jews who]...were no doubt reluctant to worship so far from their homes and preferred to form a new congregation..."[36] These "former members of the older congregation" may well have been veteran settlers, quite well integrated into the general English community. The status of veteran would be consistent with both the aspiration and the ability to assume leadership.

Not unlike the "uptowners," some of the early downtown congregations expressed their institutional aspirations, within a short time after their establishment, by seeking and finding accommodations in buildings of some note. Two congregations thus acquired buildings vacated by the original congregations. The Beth David, a congregation of Rumanian immigrants founded in 1888, purchased the synagogue of the Shearith Israel in 1890. The founding of the B'nai Jacob congregation in 1886 coincided with the move of the Shaar Hashomayim. In taking over the original synagogue, the B'nai Jacob seems to have also usurped the Shaar Hashomayim's role as the leading religious institution within the community of the surrounding area. The Chevra Kadisha, founded in 1893, built a synagogue with significant architectural presence ten years later while the Beth Yehuda settled, for the time being, in a renovated theatre which they nevertheless considered to be "quite a fine *shul*." The permanence which such indicators of physical presence might have been intended to convey was to be short-lived.

The first years of the second decade marked the beginning of the move out of the original enclave. Moving north rather than west, the immigrant Jewish community established residences, businesses, institutions and synagogues east and west of St. Lawrence Boulevard defining what would become known as "the immigrant corridor."

CHAPTER TWO

Here and There

The Dispersion of *Shuln* and *Shulelach*

St. Lawrence Boulevard is filled with people at all hours of the day and evening, for here are the food shops : kosher meat and fish markets, herring and delicatessen and dairy and bakery shops. Many of the store windows display Yiddish lettering. Even the Montreal City and District Bank at the corner of Pine and St. Lawrence has Yiddish lettering .... Everywhere, inside and out, Yiddish is heard...[37]

St. Lawrence Boulevard...undergoes a striking change as it crosses Mount Royal Avenue...Quite suddenly, it discards a great many of the features that mark it as the Jewish "Main Street." The stores that are located here are not so busy; many of them are French. Park Avenue has taken the place of St. Lawrence in this northern zone as the shopping and amusement centre.... [38]

–Judith Seidel

ONE FORMER RESIDENT has described these neighbourhoods as comprising a "*shtetl* within a *shtut*,"[39] a small Jewish town within the city of Montreal. Another nostalgically remembers the old neighbourhood as the "golden ghetto."[40] Though life was generally poorer, living conditions harder and more congested than today's lifestyle, all the residents' needs and services as well as friends and family were close at hand. It was a *shtetl* made up of immigrants of different towns, cities, and even countries, nevertheless, united by a common language. Yiddish was the predominant household language overriding the languages of the various home countries. Even in the early forties, when over fifty per cent of Montreal's Jewish population was Canadian born, Yiddish remained the mother tongue of over eighty percent of the population.[41] The Eastern European immigrants were also unified by the common tradition of Orthodox Judaism. Reform Judaism, as transported by German immigrants and ideologically and institutionally developed in the United States, had little impact on the Montreal and Canadian Jewish communities. On the other hand, the secular ideologies of Zionism and socialism formed a considerable part of the baggage of the Eastern European immigrant in the early part of the twentieth century. But within this densely populated Jewish "*shtetl* within a *shtut*," the polarization between the secular and the religious may not have been as marked as one might expect. The Eastern European immigrant synagogue of Montreal represented not so much a distinction between secular and religious as between the various immigrant communities.

By the late thirties the community was dispersed and developed in two areas of settlement centered on two distinct north-south arteries: St. Lawrence Boulevard and Park Avenue. While St. Lawrence remained the hub of Jewish commercial activity, the northern area became the location of significant Jewish institutions such as the Jewish Public Library, the YMHA, and several Jewish schools. Park Avenue also took on a distinctly Jewish character following the services of the High Holidays as the street would fill with people, mostly young, strolling from Mount Royal Boulevard to Bernard Avenue eager to socialize while wearing their best holiday attire.[42]

The community's synagogues lined the streets and boulevards east and west of Park Avenue and St. Lawrence Boulevard. Sometimes two and three to a block, or just around the corner from each other, they served a community whose population had grown significantly in the first decades of the century. In 1901 the Jewish population of Montreal, Outremont, and Westmount combined was about 8,000. By 1941 it had risen to over 63,000.[43] In 1900 approximately eight congregations served the Montreal community. By 1940 Montreal had some 45 synagogues. While the population had risen by over 680 per cent, the number of congregations had increased by only about 460 per cent. But 31 of the synagogues were concentrated in the immigrant neighbourhoods in an area of a mere two square kilometres.[44] This pales in comparison with the synagogues of New York's Lower East Side, an area of not more than two square miles, where 500 congregations had been organized in the period between 1880 and 1915.[45] How can we understand the number of synagogues relative to the population size and needs? The answer is perhaps more anecdotal than numerical.

On Shabbat the synagogues were not full. The exigencies of life in America meant that Jews had to compromise religious practices as he or she was often required to work on the Sabbath. The more observant sought work that would allow them to keep the Sabbath—either within industrial work such as the needle trade, where shops were closed on Saturday, or within the Jewish economy itself as teachers, *shochtim*, or rabbis. On a daily basis, these synagogues were certainly under-used.[46] Reuven Brasloff described the efforts of some smaller synagogues in attaining a quorum for daily prayer:

> The Plateau had many little synagogues. The problem for these synagogues was in obtaining weekday *minyans*. This became an obstacle course for my friend Benny and me on our way to school. The *shamashim* of these little synagogues would get out on the street and begin corralling anyone who looked like a Jew.[47]

On the High Holidays the synagogues were full and even overflowing as outside halls were rented and rabbis were brought in creating once-a-year synagogues for the overflow crowds. Yet one newspaper article, written in 1934 on behalf of the *Vaad Ha'ir*, suggests that even on these popular holidays, there was considerable competition and concern regarding the sale of seats and a reminder that there is no lack of seating in the permanent *shuln*. The writer makes a "heartfelt request and plea from the *Vaad Ha'ir* to all Montreal Jews to support our synagogues by going to worship on the High Holidays only in the synagogues. There is enough room in our synagogues to comfortably seat all the Jews in Montreal with their wives and children."[48]

The relative plethora of orthodox synagogues does not indicate the presence of a particularly pious community. Professor Ira Robinson, whose expertise includes, among other topics, the history of the Montreal Jewish community, has come to the same conclusion. Robinson noted the efforts of Rabbi Yudel Rosenberg as he sought to address and elevate the knowledge and practices of the Jewish community at large. However, "were he to address his exhortations only to the strictly observant Jews of Montreal, he would have talked differently. But then he would be talking to a practically empty room."[49]

This community of synagogues served a purpose other than purely religious. These houses of worship provided a place where the immigrant could feel ritually, culturally, and psychologically at home. Harry Stillman attended the Machzike Hadath during his youth and young adult years. Most of the congregants had come from the same area of the Ukraine and tended to be associated with left-wing political ideologies. The synagogue was "where they went almost out of habit to embrace a group of people, their own *landsleit*; they felt comfortable with their own."[50] Similarly, B.G. Sack, the first historian of Canadian Jewry, wrote that these immigrant Jews "sought to find a place to fit where they could do things in their own manner both socially and in terms of religion .... As these Jews could not adjust themselves to the existing synagogues, they decided to establish new *shuln* here and there.[51]

Israel Medres provided an amusing anecdotal explanation for how and why these synagogues came to be created. When an immigrant would come to Montreal, he would first attend an existing synagogue.

> When an immigrant began to feel at home in these congregations, he began to express opinions and to become involved

45

in the synagogue's business and procedures. With time he would come to disagreements with the president, the rabbi or the *gabbai* and he would become unhappy.... When a few such unhappy members would come together, they would begin planning a new congregation where the rules would be more democratic, where there would be a brotherly feeling, where the *alyiahs* would be more justly distributed, where more familiar people [*hamishe menshen*] would be elected to the offices of president, vice president and trustee...And in more or less such a manner were "*shuln* and *shulelach*" created by immigrant Jews in Montreal.[52]

Shul is the Yiddish word for synagogue. Derived from German, *shul* also means school, indicating the dual function of a synagogue as a house of worship and a house of study. *Shuln* is the plural and *shulelach*, the diminutive plural. Yiddish loves the diminutive. As in many languages, the diminutive in Yiddish implies a term of endearment. The pairing of these words focuses not only on the contrast in physical scale, but also immediately conveys a fondness of, and perhaps even a preference for, the small *shulelach*.

The *Shuln* Among the *Shulelach*

It was from among the congregations that had been established in the early enclave that the larger, mostly purpose-built, synagogues were constructed in the subsequent areas of settlement. Some of these early congregations were identified with their countries of origin. Thus the B'nai Jacob, established in 1886, was known as the *Russishe Shul*; the Beth David, founded two years later, was the *Rumainishe Shul*; and the Shaare Tefilah, dating from perhaps as early as 1892,[53] was also called the Austro-Hungarian Shul.

The Shaare Tefilah was perhaps the earliest congregation, and certainly the first synagogue built above Sherbrooke Street, probably by the end of the first decade of the twentieth-century. Israel Medres suggested that the surrounding blocks might have housed some of the wealthier members of the immigrant community.

The Shaare Tefilah, situated on Milton Street between Clark and
St. Laurent Boulevard, was the first synagogue built above Sherbrooke.

"The affluent Jews lived on Prince Arthur, Ontario, and other streets nearby."[54] The building was an imposing structure with architectural detailing possibly of Austrian influence. The circular elements on the peaks of the roof parapets and the stylized rays of light can be seen as decorative elements in German and Austrian synagogues and churches. The association of this motif with synagogues may stem from the image of Moses descending Mount Sinai, emanating light as he clasped the tablets of the commandments. A circle of rays often tops the tablets of the Ten Commandments in the decorative vocabulary of the *aron hakodesh*. A small attached building might have been used as a Talmud Torah for boys and part of the basement was reserved as a residence for the caretaker. Observers of the demolition of the building noted a recessed area in the basement level possibly indicating the presence of a former *mikvah*. Sara Jacobs's father, David Solomon, was instrumental in the building of the synagogue. He served as president until his death in 1918. Mrs. Jacobs recalls that while a green velvet curtain covered the gaps of the railing surrounding the women's gallery, the women's faces were not obscured and she had a clear view of her father sitting on the central *bimah* dressed in the formal attire of the President in a high silk hat and morning coat, a manner of dress and decorum probably not characteristic of most of the immigrant synagogues.[55]

The interior of the synagogue represented a typical arrangement for an Orthodox synagogue in this community. Separate seating areas were provided for the men and women, the most common architectural solution being, as in this case, a second level women's gallery, generally "U" shaped with the ends of the "U" ending at the wall above the *aron hakodesh*. On the main level—the men's section—the *bimah*, a raised platform containing a reading table upon which the Torah scrolls were unrolled, dominated the central space in front of the Torah Ark. In some synagogues there were no seats between the *bimah* and the Ark; in others, a few rows of seats were provided in this space for *kohanim*, heirs of the ancient priestly caste who have ritual functions in the synagogue liturgy.[56] Along the *mizrach*, the eastern wall, rows of seats on either side of the *aron hakodesh* were and are reserved for clergy and officers.

In the Shaare Tefilah, while the women were seated separately, neither their presence nor their line of view was completely obstructed, suggesting the recognition of the participation of women in the community of worshippers. The women's sections in medieval synagogues were often an afterthought, created in annexed rooms, or in a level under the main sanctuary. It is generally accepted that the first synagogue to have included a women's gallery, as "lateral galleries integrated within the space of the main prayer house,"[57] was the Sephardic Synagogue of Amsterdam in 1639. Perhaps the Sephardic residents of Amsterdam brought with them a practice of including woman's galleries as an integral part of a synagogue plan; scholars have concluded that the vestiges of some Spanish synagogues do suggest the presence of women's galleries incorporated into the upper level of one wall.[58] But the model of the Synagogue of Amsterdam was more likely derived from Protestant churches which were built to seat larger numbers of congregants within earshot of the minister. This design was adapted for synagogues by Christian architects. Until the advent of Reform Judaism in the early part of the nineteenth century, the galleries were separated physically and visually by high balustrades or grills. In Middle Eastern and Mediterranean countries, which were unaffected by Reform influences, and until today in the very pious communities, the *mechitzah* dividing men from women remains a full visual barrier. The subtle half-curtain was the typical device used to separate the women in these synagogues in Montreal rather than full-length screens or walls installed in other times, places, and communities.[59]

Further north, the Adath Yeshurun, established largely by Lithuanian Jews, began to build its synagogue in 1916. A simple and sturdy brick building, its façade was marked by a feature that would become the most prevalent distinguishing element of these urban synagogues, an arch inscribing a circular window depicting a *Magen David* in stained glass. Former members recall the traditional layout of the interior: the *aron hakodesh* faced by the central *bimah* and the women's balcony was decorated with simply-drawn illustrations, a practice common in Russian/Polish synagogues. Neither inspiring awe, nor conveying any sense of splendour, the interior was finished with woodwork that was rough and floored in linoleum. Yet auxiliary spaces, an office and small chapel used for daily *minyans* and study, distinguished it from smaller synagogues.[60]

The building of this synagogue represented a considerable effort for its members who were assisted by Lyon Cohen, the honorary president and chairman of the building committee. At the time Lyon Cohen was president of the Shaar Hashomayim. In assisting the Adath Yeshurun, he followed his father's example. Lazarus Cohen, a former president of the Shaar Hashomayim, had extended a loan to the Beth Yehuda congregation in 1906 for the purchase of its building. Lyon Cohen was probably the most prominent Jewish leader of Montreal of the time. A nephew of the prominent Rabbi Hirsch Cohen, Lyon Cohen was a leader, founder, and developer of multiple communal institutions, and an important and effective advocate for the immigrant community. On two occasions, he personally approached the United States and Canadian governments. In the first case he secured the arrival of 650 Jewish immigrants en route to the United States on the same day as the adoption of the quota system in 1921, under which the immigrants would have otherwise been refused. And in the second case he obtained Canadian immigration permits for 5,000 refugees from the Ukrainian pogrom who had found temporary haven in Rumania in 1923.[61] Yet Lyon Cohen was seen as both benefactor and detractor of the immigrants. The incident which accompanied the dedication of the Adath Yeshurun synagogue in 1917 highlights the paradoxical relationship between Lyon Cohen, as representative

The building of the Adath Yeshurun began in 1916. The arch inscribing a circular window with a stained-glass Star of David was a prevalent feature in Montreal synagogues.

of the "uptown" established Jewish community, and the downtown immigrants. Hirsch Wolofsky, founder and editor of the *Keneder Adler*, reported on the ruckus that ensued when Lyon Cohen attempted to deliver his dedicatory remarks. Mr. Cohen, chairman of the Manufacturers Association, was confronted by striking needle trade workers. Further turmoil was averted through the intervention of Mr. Wolofsky who "succeeded in bringing order to the assembly, persuading the strikers that it was not fitting for Jewish workers to disturb a religious ceremony."[62]

The first synagogue built in the third area of settlement, was the B'nai Jacob. The beautiful and commanding building was designed to serve and to lead the community as it moved northward. With this new building, B.G. Sack concluded, the B'nai Jacob "remained as important as before." Its basic Romanesque inspiration was reflected in rows of arched windows and the barrel-shaped roof creating a massive arch on the façade. Interestingly, the façade bears a striking resemblance not to synagogues of Russia, but to those of France. The sweeping arch over the entranceway bears a striking similarity to the synagogues of Nancy, France and the Rue de la Victoire in Paris, both designed by Jewish architect A.P. Aldrophe. This suggests that the congregation or the architect might have chosen to connect this important Jewish immigrant building with its location in a French-Canadian city. The building was designed to be a prominent part of the cityscape. A dominant circular window featuring a *magen david* and topped by tablets of the Ten Commandments mark it unabashedly as a synagogue. Large and obvious as it was, it was, nevertheless, dwarfed by nearby St. Michael's Church built in 1914-1915. It is also dominated by a massive arch over its façade and lateral wall.

Rare professional photographs of the interior of the synagogue attest to its acknowledged architectural importance. The interior had the elements of a traditional Orthodox synagogue. The main level featured a large central *bimah* with two rows of benches in front generally reserved for *kohanim*. An ornate *aron hakodesh* was topped by a large circular window with a *magen david* mirroring the window on the façade. Flanking the Ark were the traditional *mizrach* seats reserved for the officers. All the wood-work was rich and finely carved. While the exterior might connect the synagogue prominently as a public building in Montreal, the interior had an intimacy that evoked, in its decoration, themes common to Russian-Polish synagogues. The balustrade of the women's balcony was decorated with a plaster relief depicting the signs of the zodiac. Illustrations of the zodiac, often entwined in intricate floral designs, depictions of animals, and lines of Biblical texts, decorated the interiors of Eastern European synagogues,

(Top)B'nai Jacob, 172 Fairmount Avenue, was built in 1918.
(Bottom, left to right) Nancy Synagogue, 1861. Synagogue, rue de la
Victoire, Paris, 1861-1874.

Typical of Orthodox synagogues of this time, B'nai Jacob's interior is divided into a men's section in the main sanctuary and a women's gallery. A large *bimah* is positioned directly in front of the *aron hakodesh*.

most notably the walls and ceilings of the wooden synagogues of Russia and Poland. These wooden synagogues were almost certainly designed and built by Christians but the existence, even names, of Jewish mural painters is well documented.[63] Montreal immigrant synagogues continued this tradition—some remnants are still intact in the small, auspiciously named Temple Solomon, otherwise known as the Bagg Street Shul.

Astrology, a deterministic belief system, has been present in Judaism since ancient times, contested and supported by rabbis of the Talmud and medieval rabbis and philosophers. Abraham Ibn Ezra, a Hispano-Judaeo philosopher of the twelfth century, explained a Jewish response favourable to astrology: "Israel has no star as long as they observe the Torah. But if they do not observe it, the stars shall rule over them."[64] The practice of *mitzvoth* could mitigate against the fate predicted by the stars. The signs of the zodiac are associated with the months of the Jewish calendar. A symbolic system of attributes connects each sign of the zodiac with the Biblical, historic, ritual or spiritual significance of each month.[65] Even in one of today's most pious communities, Mea Shearim, Jerusalem, images of animals depict the signs of the zodiac and the tribes in the ceiling paintings of the Beit Haknesseth Hagadol. While the presence of imagery in synagogues belies the supposed Judaic injunction against it, it also exemplifies certain conventions in representation. Whereas sculpted images and the use of the human form are generally avoided, paintings and animal figures are not uncommon. The signs generally represented in human form in non-Judaic traditions, Virgo and Gemini, are often replaced by animals, as the two storks in the B'nai Jacob and the two gazelles in Temple Solomon, and the reindeer, whose masculine form rather comically represents Virgo in Temple Solomon. Sagittarius, whose symbol is the archer, is represented either as a drawn bow or as a detached hand pulling the bow.

The small Bagg Street Shul still retains the simple, folk-art illustrations of the zodiac drawn by a father and son named Shadewasser..[66]

The paintings are lent a certain Canadian character with the depictions of the bison and the reindeer. In the B'nai Jacob, in keeping with the more sophisticated and expensive character of its construction, the images are not painted but sculpted; they are executed with finesse and skill in the emerging Art Deco style by Harry Rappoport, a professional sculptor who later sculpted interior decorative elements for movie theatres in New York and Los Angeles.

As in the earlier neighborhood, the B'nai Jacob served as the locale for many communal gatherings including addresses by local politicians. Along with three or four other synagogues, it was the location of larger weddings and bar mitzvahs. It was known as a choral synagogue, its fine acoustics and renowned cantor attracting loyal listeners. Many young boys found their connection to synagogue life as members of its choir. The B'nai Jacob remained at this location until 1956 when it amalgamated with the Chevra Kadisha and moved to its present suburban location. Remarking on its move, perhaps regrettable though necessary, historian B.G. Sack wrote:

> [T]here are many reasons why we should maintain the old shul. We have to maintain a house of prayer whose very walls represent a sort of historic continuity that reminds us of the pioneers of yesterday and of a piece of the Jewish past of Montreal.[67]

The presence of such imposing synagogues as the Shaare Tefilah, the Adath Yeshurun, and certainly the B'nai Jacob suggests that the more established congregations had accumulated sufficient wealth to afford the expense of larger, more elaborate buildings. However, if the history of the Beth Yehuda is any indication, these buildings speak more to aspirations than to affordability. On the occasion of the fiftieth anniversary the history of the congregation was reconstructed in great detail from the archives of the synagogue and from recollections of older members

Temple Solomon, also known as the Bagg Street Shul, still retains the simple, folk-art illustrations of the zodiac that have a distinct Canadian character. (Top) Sagittarius, *keshet, Kislev*. (Bottom) Virgo, *bitulah, Elul*.

(Top) Gemini, *tiumim*, *Sivan*. (Bottom) Taurus, *shor*, *Ivar*.

and activists. The history reveals a focus on attaining a suitable building, yet the minutes record that even renovations to the original building were often an unaffordable expense. "[I]n the treasury there was not even one cent.... The officers of the time sought to beautify the synagogue. Of course, this all cost money, which wasn't there, and they were constantly appealing to the members who always did their best to respond to the requests of the officers."[68]

With the movement of the community further north, the desire and need for a new building intensified and was finally realized in 1923 when the congregation moved from its original location below Sherbrooke to its newly constructed synagogue on the eastern boundary of the second area of settlement. The congregation recorded that "[i]n that year the large and beautiful synagogue was built with all the improvements and with splendour and glory. Neither effort nor money was spared. We erected such a fine building that it was the pride of all Montreal Jews. Nearly all of the members of the shul participated in this undertaking under the leadership of the officers of the time."[69]

Not only the officers of that time, and of that particularly significant effort, but also the officers of every year and all members of every committee are listed with care and with pride. These lists comprise a "genealogy" of institution building within which the writer, Gidaliyahu Michalovsky, with somewhat less than complete modesty, includes himself as the president who ushered in "a new era in the history of the synagogue," one of greater fiscal responsibility. Yet despite his efforts and creative fundraising endeavours, the synagogue remained in financial difficulties. No sooner was it erected than it was placed on a "sheriff's sale" due to unpaid bills to contractors, and rescued thanks to the intervention of several generous members—a situation which reoccurred with alarming frequency.

With the opening of the new synagogue, and, at least partly in response to its financial difficulties, a women's auxiliary was organized. Their first event was a bazaar which culminated in a raffle offering a car as grand prize. And in the meanwhile at least, "money came in from all sides." With such a beautiful new *shul*, the congregation aspired as well to have a suitably fine cantor. "[A]nd, indeed one of the greatest cantors in the world was hired, Cantor Takach from Holland, along with a fine choir. This treat cost almost $7,000 a year." The congregation, burdened by an expensive building, was vulnerable not only to economic fluctuations, but also to the constantly changing residential patterns of its members. When Mr. Michalovsky took office in 1929 he noted that even more serious than the stock market crash was the movement away from the neighbourhood of the wealthier members and seat holders who left the synagogue a "widow" with deficits, debts, and expenses.

The need to raise funds was an ongoing enterprise. The Beth Yehuda became well-known for its cantors and cantorial concerts which were often significant fundraisers. Well known cantors, frequently from the United States, were invited to serve during the High Holidays. Presenting a concert before the holidays would not only bring in revenue, but also encourage the purchase of seats for holiday services. The performances of one rather young cantor proved to be particularly successful. Following a warning of a bank foreclosure in 1934, Mr. Michalovsky suggested that a cantor be hired for Saturdays and special concerts. When the first two cantors proved to be a disappointing draw, it was decided to bring in Cantor Shloimele, an eleven-year-old prodigy. The young cantor was engaged to sing for the High Holidays. "It was an event that brought a smile to the face of every member." The enterprise with Cantor Shloimele brought in a profit of $4,000, four times the amount that had been raised in their previously most successful concert!

The Beth Yehuda, rising several stories above its surrounding buildings, was, indeed, renowned for its splendour. Marked by a circular window with a *magan david* in stained glass on both the

(Top and bottom) The Beth Yehuda, 214 Duluth East, towered over the neighbourhood. At the rear of the building are the traces of what was once the large circular stained-glass Star of David window.

façade and rear elevation and a peaked roof topped by the tablets of the Ten Commandments, it stood proudly as a synagogue within the immediate urban landscape. A newspaper notice heralded the soon to be completed building "as one of the most beautiful synagogues in Canada." The building did not reflect any particular architectural innovation; the style could be seen not only in European synagogue prototypes, but in Montreal church architecture as well. Its distinguished façade was matched by its plush interior. Rows of circular clerestory windows on both sides would have flooded the interior with rays of coloured light streaming in with both the setting and the rising sun. As one of the grander synagogues, it was a frequent choice for larger weddings and bar-mitzvahs. The decades-long aspirations resulted in the creation of a grand locale which served the Montreal Jewish community, but the members themselves remained servants to their building.

Unfortunately, such similarly detailed accounts are not available for the other large congregations. Although the Beth Yehuda may have chosen an especially poor location for its permanent building, there is reason to believe, as we will see, that other congregations may have encountered similar difficulties in maintaining their large buildings.

The *Shulelach*

With increased immigration, smaller congregations were formed, many representing not countries of origin but geographic areas, cities, and towns as reflected in several of the names: Anshei Galicia, Ukraina, Moroshe, Ozeroff, and the Pinsker Shul. With these close ties to more recent places of origin, they remained, perhaps, more intimately connected to the places, brethren, and particular traditions which were left behind. The congregations were engaged in helping their friends and families at home, and were committed to assisting their immigration to Canada, and their integration when they arrived.

Original documents and oral histories suggest that there were varying, even conflicting, perspectives about the role that these synagogues played in the immigrant community. Formally, comments from some of the congregational leaders suggest that these small synagogues were models of stalwart orthodoxy. Organizationally they sought to both exert control over and to care for their community of members. Individually, the members were drawn to these *shuln* as an extension of *landsmanshaftn*, a connection to home, and a place where extended family and old friends could meet.

RELIGIOUS AND SOCIAL FUNCTIONS

> [L]et us praise the value of the small *shulelach* that maintain the true traditional Judaism without deviation and without modernization.[70]

Such were the words of praise of Rabbi Yehoshua Halevi Herschorn, his words echoed by the comments of others, on the occasion of the twenty-fifth anniversary of the Anshei Ozeroff. Special occasions provided an opportunity for communal recognition of the small congregations. On the occasion of the eightieth birthday of Rabbi Hirsch Cohen and celebration of his fiftieth anniversary of residence in Montreal in 1940, several smaller congregations paid tribute to him as well as to themselves. Their sentiments were recorded in a souvenir booklet of the event. *Zerei Dath V'doath*, Young Men of Religion and Learning, as the name indicates, was established for the dual purpose of prayer and study. "Until this day," they proclaimed "every *Shabbos*, before prayers, they study an hour of *shulchan aruch* or *gemara*." Likewise, a representative of the Tifereth Israel wrote: "The synagogue conducts itself according to the most beautiful, traditional ways and is firmly based in the foundations of Torah and charity. We worship and study every day and we support Jewish institutions of justice and Torah." Baruch Tannenbaum, president of Machzike Hadath, extolled his synagogue: "Though [the *shul*] is small, it had always taken an active role in all orthodox and religious matters and supports, with all her efforts, Talmud scholars…"[71]

Yet it is unlikely that President Tannenbaum's vision of the Machzike Hadath as a leading Orthodox institution in the Jewish community was a motivating factor for its congregants. What drew the members to this *shul*, whether on Shabbath or on holidays, was a sense of familiarity. Most of the congregants came from the same area of the Ukraine, from Kaminetz-Podolsk, and from the towns of Dinovitz and Poskurov. Harry Stillman noted its significance as being "more of a *landsleit* type of association than a religious one," its members being for the most part, not particularly religious. Similarly, Percy Tannenbaum,[72] a nephew of Baruch, noted that his parents were Labour Zionists. For his grandfather, who attended services every morning, the *shul* served a satisfying social function. On nice days, he and his friends and fellow worshippers would convene in Fletcher's Field or Marie-Anne Park. President Tannenbaum's children were not educated in religious schools, in *cheders* or Talmud Torah, but in the Folkshule, the Jewish People's School with a Labour-Zionist orientation. His daughter Rose Tannenbaum Zuckerman recalls that, though her parents both went to *shul* on *Shabbos*, the children did not. Yet gatherings in their home on holidays and every *Shabbos* remain memorable.

Yolette Vool Mendleson described a similar connection to the Pinsker Shul which was founded by immigrants from Pinsk, Poland, her great-uncle among them. She too attended the Folkshule which served as a focal point of family involvement and an expression of their Labour-Zionist orientation. The household was kosher, the holidays were celebrated in a traditional manner, and though her father worked on most Saturdays, he would attend *shul* on a *Shabbos* when he wasn't working. Their home provided a welcoming haven for recently arrived immigrants, a hub for political discussions, and a gathering place for the *landsleit* following holiday services. Her memories of the synagogue itself convey a sense of warmth and familiarity.

I remember it in connection with the holidays and everyone together and having a good time. I would visit my mother upstairs and see all the cousins. It was stuffy and hot....The decorum was lively and noisy. Quiet was often asked for. The women would pray but there was also a lot of conversation with kids running in and out.[73]

The members of the Anshei Ukraina seemed particularly closely connected, bound by a shared memory that was both poignant and enduring. When the congregation received its charter in 1924, it registered a name that served as appellation and mission: "Anshei Ukraina, in memory of the holy ones who were martyred in the Ukraine." The members of the congregation formed an extended social group and the *shul* was the focal point of the community on any given Saturday. "If you needed anyone for anything important during *Shabbos*," Olive Golick Brumer relates, "you would go to the synagogue." Informal discussions and gatherings continued after services and on Sundays. Though some of the meetings were on the financial matters of the *shul*, often a newcomer would be invited to speak, as the members were anxious to hear news from home.

If it was heard that an immigrant came from the Ukraine he would be encouraged to come to the *shul*. One told the other. It was something that would attach them to home. And they would have an understanding of what it meant to escape from a pogrom.[74]

The sense of mutual responsibility conveyed by the comments of former members of these small congregations is also suggested in the texts of a handful of surviving documents. On the occasion of the twenty-fifth anniversary of the Anshei Ozeroff, Sam Birenbaum, secretary of the congregation for seventeen years, noted with pride this tradition of caring for the members here and *landsleit* in Ozeroff. He describes that while money was collected to buy a new Torah scroll and to assist members in need, the congregation was "not indifferent to the cry for help from our home town…and an additional considerable sum was sent to our *shtetl*, Ozeroff.[75]

On the occasion of the tribute evening for Rabbi Hirsch Cohen, the leaders of the Anshei Ukraina recalled their own bitter past in Europe, their dedication to their "brothers and sisters," and their commitment to maintaining traditional values in Montreal.

> As fate had it, we settled in Montreal where daily life with its "*Hoo-Ha*" was ready to swallow us together with our memories and obligations to our brothers and sisters. Eventually, some of us, who understood the danger of the situation, undertook to initiate the organization of an administrative body empowered to organize the newly arrived refugees with the goal of helping one another in the time of need as well as to support friends and acquaintances overseas…[76]

It would seem that the "Hoo-Ha" of daily life in Montreal, if we can take that to mean the temptation of Canadianization, posed nearly as great a danger of eliminating collective memory and values as did the pogroms. The solution was not only to help each other, those who had arrived and those who were still overseas, but also to establish an organization, a *shul*, by which the process of integration could be mitigated against and controlled.

Very few documents, as the one quoted above have survived. From several announcements of meetings, a minute book, the vestiges of a revised constitution, and an anniversary souvenir book, we can piece together the sense of responsibility and mission of the many small synagogues. The announcements of meetings all followed a similar format. Addressed to a "worthy brother" they indicated the agenda of the meeting, usually the installation of officers and presentation of the annual report, and provided a space indicating the sums which the member still owed the synagogue in membership fees, contribution to the building fund or charity fund. Punitive measures were directed at those who fell in arrears, but at the same time a charity fund was set up to extend loans to needy "brothers." Everyone was encouraged to bring in new members to help maintain and increase the congregations. Announcements of meetings of the Hadrath Kodesh congregation included a letterhead logo depicting two hands clasped in brotherhood. During the late twenties and thirties, not surprisingly, the announcements expressed an ongoing financial concern. Apparently by the thirties a ladies' auxiliary had been organized as one of the notice of meetings encourages the "brothers" to see to it that their wives were registered. The establishment of ladies' auxiliaries seems to be consistent with economic difficulties as they provided not only a social diversion for the women but also maintained fundraising efforts. One meeting in 1931 was organized for a particularly poignant purpose suggesting that, small as the congregation might have been, their sense of purpose went beyond their own congregational needs. Indicative of their ongoing concern for the Jews of Europe, they met to register a collective protest with the Polish government against the relentless pogroms.

The minute book of the Anshei Ozeroff congregation, dated 1925-1943, remains extant. Embedded in it is a revised version of the congregation's constitution. Ozeroff (Ozarow) was a *shtetl* in central Poland south of Warsaw. In 1921, 2,258 Jews formed 65 per cent of the total population. The Jewish population was administered internally by an elected *kehillah*.[77] Small and poor though the community was, it nevertheless maintained several communal institutions. Coming from such a small town, it is not surprising that the administration of the congregation in Montreal became an extension of the former *kehillah,* both regulating its congregants' behaviour and caring for their needs. This essential sense of purpose and empowerment is suggested in the constitution and reinforced in the records of the minutes. Informal, and handwritten in Yiddish, as a list of points in no particular order, the constitution stands in contrast to the formally written and structured bylaws of the earlier B'nai Jacob. It does not designate consistent

Page from the Anshei Ozeroff minute book (1925-1943) pertaining to the revision of the constitution.

rules and regulations of meetings, nor does it define and enumerate the standing officers, their roles and responsibilities. But what stands out in the points of this constitution are matters auxiliary to synagogue management and conduct. Disputes between "brothers" may not be brought to a court of law before the issue is discussed by the congregation. Here the synagogue administration assumes the role of the *beit din* in a traditional Jewish community where civil legal matters were handled internally. One such dispute is recorded in the minutes. Brother Shaphir had publicly insulted Brother Green who had exhibited some form of misconduct in front of strangers near the *shul*. Following three hours of deliberation, they were each fined three dollars. More striking still are the privileges and assistance extended to members. The B'nai Jacob constitution contains a short article that lists the "rights of membership" which includes the right to distribute *aliyahs* "when a member's son has a bar mitzvah or before his wedding" and a free *chupa* for the marriage of a child of a member. The privileges granted a brother and his family at the Anshei Ozeroff show far greater concern and generosity. On the occasion of a wedding, a child of a member must be offered a gift and members of the officers are selected to attend the *simcha*. A daughter who is married following the death of her father is entitled to a free wedding and a gift. Special consideration and reduced fees are extended to the widow and unmarried minor children of a deceased member. Finally, while the minutes of the congregation attest to the ongoing struggle to meet the financial obligations of the synagogue, the constitution stipulates that "when a brother is in a critical situation, we must help him. The president and vice-president must borrow money from the *shul*, up to 25 dollars, in order to help the brother. A meeting is to be called and a tax exacted on every brother according to the decision of the meeting. The money must be collected immediately."[78]

The Anshei Ozeroff anniversary publication of 1943 was a celebration of tenacity and the particular ties that bound the members together even in the face of the massive tragedy engulfing their brethren trapped in Poland. The small size of the institution and shared background of the congregants certainly enhanced the sense of belonging and mutual responsibility. As some of the texts suggest, smallness was also a symbol of traditionalism and insurance against assimilation. Several external community leaders were invited to contribute articles to the anniversary publication addressing the quality of smallness not merely as a virtue but as a metaphor of virtue.

> There is a Talmudic legend that when the Temple was destroyed, God spread the stones over the entire world and on every place where a stone landed, a synagogue was built. Hence, every synagogue is called a small temple—a *mikdash miat.*[79]

Though *mikdash miat* refers to all synagogues, large and small, as the institutional heirs of the destroyed Temple, one senses that the writer speaks of a small synagogue when using this term as a metaphor for the Anshei Ozeroff.

Rabbi Yehoshua Halevi Herschorn proclaims the virtues of a small synagogue in terms that are far more explicit and directly critical of large synagogues. He aims barbed language directly at the "[Reform] temples and conservative synagogues whose members belong to the "high windows." [An expression meaning auspicious and wealthy buildings or high positions.] This includes those orthodox synagogues who have comfortable large buildings and who boast about whatever they have. A small *shul* has no chance against such honor." Rabbi Herschorn quite clearly attacks the larger synagogues on two fronts: conspicuous and unaffordable expenditures and dilution of orthodox practice. "Our parents in Lithuania, Poland, the Ukraine, Rumania, and Hungary," he wrote "used to pray in houses of study, small prayer groups, *shtibles,* and small synagogues that distinguished themselves not with greatness of buildings and not with beautiful accommodations."

The Anshei Ozeroff's Silver Jubilee Anniversary publication, 1943.

Immigrants falsely believed that only large and beautiful buildings could attract youth to synagogue. This unsuccessful strategy left them with nothing but "large mortgages and debts." The synagogue is saved from financial ruin only through the generosity "of a good president or treasurer who reaches into his own pocket and the balance must be raised by the brothers..." The large building in itself necessitates a constant search for more members and thus the congregation looks "in other false directions." They "anglicize" and "modernize" the service and try to establish attractive new programs.

> When the future historian will examine the mistakes that the early Jewish inhabitants made (if such a historian will one day exist), he will not fail to note the mistake that was made that through grand buildings, beautiful walls and carpets...
>
> And as such errors are only to be found in the large synagogues, let us praise the value of the small *shulelach* that maintain the true traditional Judaism without deviation and without modernization.[80]

Conflict and Change in Europe

Rabbi Herschorn's nostalgia for the small synagogues of "Lithuania, Poland, the Ukraine, Rumania, and Hungary" belies the fact that the cities of nineteenth-century Europe witnessed the construction of monumental synagogues which dwarfed any built in Montreal. The granting of citizenship for Jews and the abolition of residential restrictions was accompanied by a dramatic migration from rural to urban centres in Western and Central Europe. But the building of the large synagogues often preceded the dates of full emancipation and, as Professor Richard Cohen has pointed out, also often preceded the period of largest growth of the population.[81] In Eastern Europe large synagogues were built in anticipation of emancipation which never fully materialized. These prominent structures were clearly an expression of optimism and a "demand to be visible."[82] Not all Jews, however, greeted the project of the construction of opulent synagogues with equal enthusiasm. In Carol Herselles Krinsky's summary of the development of large synagogues in modern Europe, we hear the echo of Montreal's Rabbi Herschorn's concerns:

> Traditionalists ...were concerned about the spiritual danger if they imitated the practice of building large churches. They knew that assimilation in general culture and assimilation in architecture often went together...
>
> Jews who wanted to confirm their place in modern society built large synagogues that would, as they put it, be worthy of their cities and show the congregations' gratitude for their new civil status.[83]

Actual examples of advocacy and opposition reveal even greater tension than the description portrayed by Krinsky. The confrontation between Hasidim and Maskilim in nineteenth-century Galicia, thoroughly documented by Raphael Mahler,[84] provides a rather extreme example of conflict between assimilationists and traditionalists. Joseph Perl led the Maskilim in virtual battle against the Hasidim. Sharing the values of the absolute monarchs, who sought to centralize their powers by eliminating the ethnic differences among their subjects, the Maskilim promoted secular education and disdained the irrational practices of Hasidism. Perl petitioned the authorities to confiscate "harmful books, close Hasidic *battei midrash*, and *minyamim*...[as places] of refuge for vagabonds, thieves, and similar types and, as a matter of course, a nest of demoralization and of harmful, often even nefarious, scandalous deeds."[85] A note attached by the provincial governor to Perl's petition to the emperor described Perl as "one of the most educated men of his nation, the founder of the great synagogue, that is, the temple in Tarnopol."[86] The conflict between Perl and the Hasidim came to a head in Tarnopol when Perl appointed a *maskilic* rabbi to the pulpit of the main synagogue. The Hasidim responded by desecrating the synagogue, inscribing a prohibition to the devoted on the wall of the building: "Thou shalt utterly detest it, and thou shalt utterly abhor it; for it is a cursed thing." They went so far as to violate the most sacred space, the *aron hakodesh*, "with mud and pitch."[87] The level of mutual animosity is most vividly described in a contemporary report of Perl's funeral. The coffin was followed by municipal and district officials and by "armed police agents who were dispatched to guard the corpse against an attack by Hasidim. On Perl's fresh grave the Hasidim let loose in a wild dance."[88]

The founders of the great Tlomackie Synagogue built in Warsaw from 1874-1877 were described in Alexander Guterman's essay as enlightened and acculturated Jews. They sought integration but, reluctant to forgo attachments to traditional Judaism, rejected Reform. The more Orthodox, nevertheless, shunned this synagogue and referred to it as "*di daytche schul*," the German Shul, its members little better than *goyim*. A contemporary journalist wrote: "At the time, the strictly observant circles of the Hasidim considered the 'Synaogoga' itself an impure place, where no Jew who had not shed his Judaism (*a yiddisher yid*) could show his face, particularly not to pray..."[89] Indeed, the Hasidic prayer house remained the prevalent model of Jewish space of worship in Warsaw which had, as Krinsky notes, 450 *shtibels* by 1926.

The synagogue of the Progressive Jews of Lodz (1881), modelled after and rivalling the Tlomackie Synagogue in scale and grandeur, was similarly known as the German Shul. Author Krzysztof Stefanski wrote that the wealthy "manufacturers, merchants, and bankers" who founded the synagogue were also called "'civilized' or 'German-ritual' Jews not because their ritual followed the German tradition, but because they derived assimilationist patterns from Germany."[90]

The first country to grant equal citizenship to the Jews was France in 1791. The Jewish communities were organized under official *consistories*. Conflict ensued throughout the course of the latter half of the nineteenth century between the Jewish authorities of the *consistoire* of Paris and the growing population of Eastern European immigrants. The *consistoire* was represented by the monumental Rue de la Victoire synagogue built in 1875 in the Romanesque style. The Eastern European immigrants worshipped, as they had in Eastern Europe, in a plethora of small prayer rooms. The communal leadership battled these private *minyamim*, enlisting, as in Galicia, government support in controlling their dispersion. In 1911 nine small congregations did merge to build a substantial synagogue of their own. Some scholars have suggested their choice of a divergent and original style indicated a form of resistance and a statement of independence from the established community.[91] The young architect Hector Guimard was enlisted to build in the then current and innovative Art Nouveau style. The interior layout of the synagogue on Rue Pavé, with clearly separate demarcation of space between *bimah* and *aron hakodesh*, remained entirely Orthodox. But the statement of the president of the new congregation indicates that "large," in itself, represented change and modernization.

> We no longer need to take refuge in temporary, private premises where our children refuse to accompany us. We shall have a large synagogue with all modern conveniences.[92]

HUMBLE BUILDINGS

In contrast, the synagogue that Montreal's Anshei Ozeroff dedicated in 1943 on the occasion of the twenty-fifth anniversary of the congregation, was a simple building. Despite the title of the souvenir book which announces the "Opening of Our Newly Erected Synagogue," the building was a former residential building, one of two identical units in a series of row houses typical in Montreal's urban landscape. The interior was renovated to accommodate the necessary fittings of a synagogue including a second level women's gallery. The *bimah* and the Ark were well carved. The synagogue's secretary, Sam Birenbaum, a frequent *bal tefilah* and *bal kore* (a lay leader of prayers and reader of the Torah) was

(Top) The former Anshei Ozeroff, 5244 St. Urbain Street, one of a twin in a series of rowhouses.
(Bottom) Sam Birenbaum, unknown, Max Gorman, and Edward Shaffer standing in front of the synagogue entrance.

a carpenter by trade who had hand-carved two lions which perched above the *aron hakodesh*. An extension to the rear of the building accommodated the Ark which was illuminated by a circular window still visible on the rear elevation. A rare photo of members standing in front of the building, including Mr. Birenbaum and other "brothers," bears evidence that only the door, with the name of the congregation in wood relief and a small circular window with a stained-glass *magen david*, marked the building as a synagogue.

The large majority of the buildings which served as synagogues in these old Jewish neighbourhoods were converted from existing buildings. Not more than four of the small *shuls* were purpose-built. Two of these, north of the area of greatest concentration, the Poele Zedek and the Tifereth Jerusalem, were built by the members themselves. Jewish craftsmen, carpenters, plumbers, and electricians dedicated several years of their after-work hours to build their own houses of worship. But even those created on the base of pre-existing buildings featured architectural elements that clearly identified them as synagogues. The Nusach Ha'ari provides an excellent example.[93]

Former members recall the conversion of the duplex into a synagogue. The congregation originally worshipped on the ground floor. A curtain in the back divided the women from the men. The upstairs was a separate apartment. In 1947 the congregation took over the upper unit and completely renovated the building, creating a typical small synagogue. The symmetrical façade is marked by a two-storey concrete arch with an inscribed circular window with a stained glass *magen david* and the exposed lateral wall was fitted with a row of stained-glass windows. The entrance is punctuated by a peaked parapet decorated with a row of arches formed by brickwork, a prevalent "neo-Romanesque" motif of both Montreal synagogues and churches of the early twentieth-century. Double entrance doors lead into a small vestibule. On the right a stairway leads up to the women's gallery created from the former second floor of the duplex. A second set of doors opens

Tifereth Jerusalem, 6627 Cartier Street, was built in 1911.

up onto the main sanctuary. A Talmudic passage (b. Berakoth 8a) calls for two doors as entrance to a synagogue which has often been interpreted as a door from the outside into the vestibule and a second door from the vestibule into the sanctuary.[94] The vestibule serves as a transition between the mundane and the spiritual. The lower height of the vestibule ceiling, often imposed by the floor of the gallery above, creates a sense of grandeur, even in the smallest synagogues, as the worshipper passes into the main sanctuary. The vestibule, directly aligned to the axis of *bimah* and *aron hakodesh*, also introduces a reference to the ancient Temple and the procession of chambers leading to the Holy of Holies, which, it is said, the priests accessed through a series of veils to reveal the Tabernacle. In the synagogue the mystery of the Holy of Holies is encapsulated in the *aron hakodesh*. In this synagogue the Ark is built into a niche extended from the rear of the building. A designated reader climbs the steps to the Ark as the Talmud stipulates that men should go down from it.[95] He pushes aside the Torah curtain (*parochet*), opens the doors of the cabinet, removes the silver ornamentation, shield (*tas*), crown (*keter*), and finials (*rimonim*), and pulls away the velvet sleeve which covers the scroll. Finally placing it on the reading table of the *bimah*, the *bal koreh*, the lay reader of the Torah text, unravels the scroll to the designated weekly portion, and guiding his eyes with a silver pointer (*yad*), begins to read the sacred text.

The focus is now on the *bimah* and the reader. These small congregations generally did not have their own clergy. Sometimes one rabbi would have an association with several small congregations, visiting them occasionally to deliver a *drash*, an interpretation of Torah or Talmud. These rabbis would rarely receive remuneration, earning their living instead as *mohelim* or *schochtim*. Cantorial music was highly valued and sometimes a visiting cantor would draw crowds even to the small *shuln*. The services, however, were generally conducted by the congregants themselves.

The sanctuary of the Nusach Ha'ari is sombre, save for sunny days when light streams in through the stained glass windows. The woodwork of the Ark and the traditional *bimah* is dark and richly ornamented. Both the Ark and *bimah* were built by the congregation's major benefactor and president, a furniture manufacturer, Morris Gorelik. This synagogue also probably represents an average size for the congregations in this area, or what might be considered a medium-sized synagogue. It seats about two hundred men on the main level and about ninety women in the gallery. One can make an interesting observation about the direction of prayer in this synagogue. The direction of prayer is mandated to be towards Jerusalem. Therefore, in the West, the *aron hakodesh*, housing the Torah scrolls, should be on the eastern or *mizrach* wall. Yet this injunction regarding the direction of prayer seems to have often been ignored in orienting these houses of worship. Only about a third face east.[96] In the Nusach Ha'ari the direction

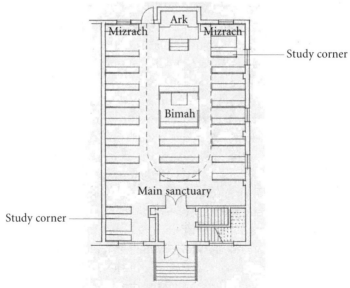

(Top) Nusach Ha'ari, 5538 Jeanne-Mance Street, was constructed in 1947. (Bottom) Floorplan of the synagogue.

of prayer seems to have been taken quite seriously. The benches along the *mizrach* wall are reserved for the synagogue officers and face out towards the congregation. Not only does the rear of the building face east, but the *mizrach* benches have a shelf that lifts up from the back allowing the worshipper to rest his book while turning to face east during standing prayers.

In Judaism the task of study and learning is complimentary to prayer. A place for learning forms part of the interior spatial requirements of a traditional synagogue. The basement, lined with shelves of decaying books, was once used as a study hall and retains its function as a *kiddish* room. In the main sanctuary, tables and benches line the wall in front of the *mizrach* seats. And in the rear of the sanctuary, in a space fitted with an armoire of books, a table and chairs, a study corner is illuminated by the filtered light of stained glass. One former member recalls the ambiance in the *shul* as day turned to dusk during the study sessions between the afternoon and evening prayers.

> Between *mincha* and *maariv* services, there was always a period of "*lernen.*" [study] The men would sit around a table beside the *aron hakodesh*. There was a bench against the wall and chairs around it. [The rabbi] would read the Hebrew and then translate into Yiddish and the men would argue points of law. With the announcement by one of the men that the first star was in the sky we would *daven maariv* and then go home.[97]

Unlike the Nusach Ha'ari, most of the small congregations were housed in premises that probably underwent little renovation in their transformation to a synagogue. Walking the neighbourhood today there are few signs remaining of what once was a synagogue in a triplex, duplex, or commercial loft. Only the rare photo or the recollections of a former worshipper provide clues as to how these buildings might have been adapted to serve as small *shuln*. The building which once housed the Kerem Israel is a simple two storey brick residential unit with modern rectangular windows. A photo in the hands of the Parnass family, who once owned the synagogue, reveals that a simple arch with an inscribed *magen david* once extended above the roof cornice. The name of the congregation and the date of its foundation, 1910, are engraved above the entranceway. The congregation worshipped on the ground floor while the second floor was used not as a women's gallery but as a free school for children. The Stepener Shul was housed in an attached cottage that had previously served as the fifth home of the Jewish Public Library. Photographs from the Library's archives reveal stained-glass windows featuring *magen davids* on the double doors. It is reasonable to assume that the Stepener Shul maintained these glass panels. According to the current resident who purchased the building from the congregation, the second level was open to the lower level, indicating

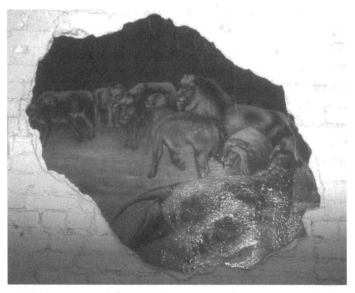

Remnant of the original wall mural from the Stepener Shul,
4115 St. Urbain.

(Top and middle) Kerem Israel, 4335 St. Dominique, was constructed in 1910. (Bottom) Architect Harry Stillman's drawing of the synagogue east of what is now the Parc du Portugal.

The Stepener Shul, 1978, 4115 St. Urbain, was housed in an attached cottage that had previously served as the fifth home of the Jewish Public Library.

that the congregation had renovated the space to form a women's gallery. The current owner retained a small section of a plaster wall with a wall painting depicting a cluster of lions which once formed a larger mural painted by the congregation.

Congregations worshipping in commercial premises probably did very little to alter the space. The furnishings, including a simple *aron hakodesh* and an equally plain *bimah*, were probably portable. These spaces may have been provided by a fellow congregant or other community member who owned the building. Such was the case with the Shevet Achim, whose congregants were allowed to worship rent-free by Abraham Ragninsky, a conscientious community leader who was then the president of the B'nai Jacob. As a result "...it was decided that because Mr. Ragninsky had done so much for us...that the name be changed to Shevet Achim d'Bet Avraham."[98]

Today, many former residents refer to all the small *shuln* in the old neighbourhoods as *shtibels*. There is probably more than just a touch of nostalgia in so broadly defining all the small places of worship. Perhaps we can arrive at a more accurate social and architectural definition of a *shtibel*. *Shtibel* means small house or room. In the European context of the *shtetl*, a *shtibel* might have been a small free-standing house or simply a place designated for prayer and study in someone's home. The following description of the *shtibel* in Lodz, Poland could equally serve as a description of those re-established in Montreal.

> [The *shtiblen*] were more often than not simply converted living accommodations in which the *aron hakodesh* was placed along with a temporary *bimah*. Usually the faithful sat on tables rather than on benches. Worship was conducted often by laymen. The adherents of various tzaddiks [spiritual leaders] had their own houses of worship which were concentrated where Hasids lived. The Hasidic *shtibel* was not only a place of prayer where rabbinical teachings were conducted. It was not only Hasids who worshipped in houses of prayer; they were equally founded by neighbourhood groups from several houses of the same street.[99]

The combination of prayer and study in an intimate setting reserved, probably exclusively for men, is what characterize a *shtibel*. In the Hasidic tradition a *shtibel* was formed around a local charismatic *rebbe*. In the Montreal setting a *shtibel* might have been as simple as a *minyan* of men worshiping in someone's home or commercial premises. The Zerei Dath V'Doath congregation worshipped in a series of commercial and residential sites. One of their locations occupied the first floor of an attached duplex which they converted into a sanctuary and study hall with little or no alteration to the former interior configuration. The former hallway, living room, and dining room served as the space for the sanctuary while the kitchen space was used as an afternoon chapel. A rear door led out to a small yard in which a *succah* with a retractable roof was erected during Succoth. Small as it may have been, the sanctuary had the necessary fittings of a traditional synagogue: a central *bimah* and an *aron hakodesh* on the eastern wall which was flanked by chairs for the officers and the honorary *mizrach* seats. However, instead of rows of fixed benches, arranged from side to side, the small sanctuary was fitted with tables and benches, placed front to back. In such a configuration study partners could face each other and discuss points of law or Biblical interpretations. This indicated a dual function of *beit tefillah* (house of prayer) and *beit midrash* (house of study). Such a configuration allowed for no women's section. Within the architectural context of this neighbourhood of Montreal, this could most clearly be called a *shtibel*, a small house of prayer and study which did not generally include the participation of women. This congregation continues to worship in a small converted residential building in the Côte-des-Neiges area, an area of subsequent migration of the Jewish community.

The Tallner Beit Hamidrash could also be considered a *shtibel*, in this case, formed in the early forties around a Hasidic rabbi, Rabbi Twersky, who was supported entirely by his congregants. A small cottage provided a residence for the rabbi and his family on

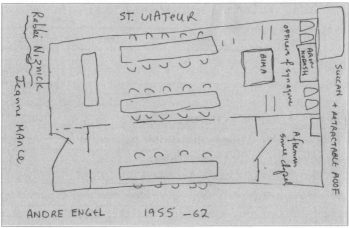

The lower floor of this corner triplex, 5457 Jeanne-Mance, once housed Zerei Dath V'Doath. The monumental St. Michael's Church looms in the background. The floor plan sketch was drawn from memory by Andre Engel, a congregant in the years 1955-1962.

the second floor with the *shtibel* on the ground floor. Ben Zion Dalfen, a former congregant, described the use and configuration of the space.

> There were about sixty or seventy men congregants and a women's section behind a *mechitzah* on the same floor which held about thirty women. Yet the women came rarely. The *rebitzin* would be there and maybe five or six others and during Yom Tov [there would be more].... The "sanctuary" was the former living room and dining room. The only thing that was posted on the wall was the *luach*, with dates of all the holidays. Nothing else adorned the interior and nothing marked the *shul* on the exterior.[100]

Small weddings and bar mitzvahs of no more than a hundred guests were held in the sanctuary. The central *bimah* was moved aside, tables and benches were rearranged, and food brought out from the small kitchen.

The women, not included in study and minimally in worship, were called into service in the preparation of receptions and holiday meals. Unlike the *shtibel*, however, most of even the smallest synagogues had a designated women's section, often created by opening the ceiling to the second floor to form the traditional women's gallery. Yet, by most accounts, the women's sections were not full except on the High Holidays.

The presence of ladies' auxiliaries in many of these congregations suggests, however, that synagogue life served an important social function for women and that they made a necessary contribution to the financial needs of their congregations. The still extant cornerstone of the Anshei Ukraina acknowledges the role of the ladies' auxiliary in the construction of the synagogue. In traditional Judaism the role of the woman is in the home, not just as homemaker, but as provider and facilitator of many important religious and ritual functions which are fulfilled in the home. But in the case of these smaller synagogues, the home served as

The cornerstone of the Anshei Ukraina congregation. It reads:
"Ladies' Auxiliary – They also contributed to and were
occupied with the construction of this building."

an extension of the space of the synagogue. Thus the dining room
served as conference table for board meetings and planning and
social gatherings of the ladies' auxiliary; the kitchen and living
room were reception halls, welcoming worshippers after services;
and the entire house was transformed for weddings and bar mitzvahs. Writer Shulamis Yelin recalled weddings in her bubbi's house.

> The weddings of *landsleit* were celebrated in my Bubi's
> house. In the living room they had the *chuppah*. The cooking
> was done in the basement kitchen. Upstairs in the bedrooms,
> the beds were taken out. They rented tables. The daughters
> were the waitresses. Everyone helped and it was great fun.
> This happened many times. *Yontif* was *yontif* and celebration
> was celebration.

As often as weddings or celebrations came about, *Shabbos* hap-
pened every week. Then, as today in a traditional household, the
home was a swarm of activity. In the memory of Morty Bercovitch,
Shabbos preparations were "fantastic."

The house was spotless. My mother would get up at five or six in the morning and throw in a load of coal in the stove. Then she would wash and wax the floors. Then she would make her gefilte fish and her *kigels* and her *latkes* and her roasted chickens. She would bake, of course, and prepare the *cholent* for Shabbos. I would have the chore of grating the horseradish. Her chicken soup was absolutely incredible with *knaidlach* and *kreplach*....Even after we were all married *Shabbos* was still at my mother's house.

Such a meal required grating, chopping, kneading, rolling, and stuffing, all without the help of modern appliances, not to mention probably hand-plucking the chickens. It is no wonder that, as Mr. Bercovitch explained, while "the synagogue was half to three quarters full [on *Shabbos*], there were not so many women in the gallery. The women mostly stayed home." After all these preparations what woman wouldn't welcome a few hours of undisrupted quiet before hungry family and friends assembled after services?

With modest means, and in a relatively simple manner, these small synagogues, *shulelach*, and *shtibels* adapted themselves within an existing urban environment. Most were located in pre-existing buildings modified to a greater or lesser degree to accommodate the needs of a synagogue. This was not only an expression of modesty and a reflection of limited financial means, but a practical response to the situation of a membership that moved with some frequency. Many of these congregations, like the Anshei Ozeroff, had several locations over time, following their members as they moved north and west. Some, like the Shomrim Laboker, with a primary location in the southern corner of the second area of settlement, set up branches in other neighbourhoods, often within the commercial premises of a congregant. The Anshei Ukraina also moved to remain close to its congregants. To once again borrow some key words from the speech of a leader of that congregation in 1940, we recall how they sought to "keep together" to sustain a "*shul* [that] would forever carry the memory" and would guard against the "Hoo-Ha" of daily life which "was ready to swallow us together with our memories and obligations to our brothers and sisters." Smallness was not just a consequence of practicality; it was a conscious existential choice responding to a concern articulated by Rabbi Herschorn.

> The Orthodox *shul* is in danger of losing its orthodoxy and this, to a large measure, is due to the state of some of the large Orthodox synagogues....The small synagogues have not been moved by the harmful influences and, thus, they remain, until today, the minor temples that they were in the Diaspora.[101]

While the religious and lay leaders may have been concerned with maintaining traditional Eastern European Orthodoxy, the synagogues served not only as places of worship but also as gathering places where the newcomers could feel welcome, respected, and at home in their adopted country. The larger and older congregations, having aspired to and acquired larger synagogues, were less concerned with serving a congregation narrowly defined by place of origin and more focused on their leadership role within the community at large. They signified a conscious transformation from immigrant to Canadian Jew. As Herschorn said, the tendency was to "Anglicize and modernize" and thus to Canadianize. Yet even the small *shulelach*, which clung to familiar and particular traditions, nevertheless aided in integration by providing a spiritual, social, and cultural context in which the immigrant could flourish.

CHAPTER THREE

The Synagogues of the "High Windows"

In the first years after the great world war, the traditionally rich Jews, the uptowners, lost their privileged status in the community. Many of the downtowners, the former immigrants, had benefited from the wartime prosperity and also became well off, some of them even very wealthy.

Some of them moved to Outremont, which was as well [as Westmount] a fine residential neighbourhood. Soon a dense Jewish neighbourhood developed there. New streets with beautiful homes were quickly built where the former downtowners now resided who had become lucky in business and became quite well off.[102]

–Israel Medres

THREE OF THE FOUR SYNAGOGUES in the municipality of Outremont area did, indeed, have high windows. But the phrase in Yiddish is not architectural but metaphorical and refers to an area of imposing buildings. With a knowing look and a certain intonation of voice, the expression "*Er is fin di hoche fensters*"—"He is from the high windows"—would describe the social status of a person living in such an area. Three of the synagogues moved to this district within a three-year period from 1926-1929, after purchasing former churches. On the very edge of Outremont, they were located within blocks of each other in order to serve a burgeoning community. The fourth synagogue was built in 1940 in the heart of Outremont to serve as both synagogue and community centre for a, by then, well-established community.

From Church to Synagogue

When the Beth David purchased a former church in 1929, at the southeast tip of Outremont, it was positioned to serve this growing Jewish population. In relocating from Chenneville Street the Beth David took on many new members in addition to those who had followed the congregation. Lawrence "Sonny" Popliger was a young boy at the time of the move. His father, a lawyer, facilitated the purchase of the building and served as the synagogue's president for several years. His grandfather was a member of the Adath Yeshurun, a smaller and older *shul* built on St. Urbain Street in the second area of settlement in 1916.

> The Chenneville Street synagogue was comparable to the Adath Yeshurun in that they felt older and attracted an older con-gregation....The Adath Yeshurun was my grandfather's *shul*. The Beth David was my father's *shul*.[103]

The Beth David differed as well from the Adath Yeshurun and other traditional synagogues in the layout of the interior space. The building itself, the former St. Giles Presbyterian Church, was probably only slightly altered in its transformation to a synagogue. Only a plaque over the entranceway, probably featuring the tablets of the Ten Commandments, indicated the metamorphosis from church to synagogue. A traditional section for the women was adapted from the pre-existing balconies and supplemented by a section in the rear of the sanctuary. The greatest divergence from the arrangement of a traditional synagogue was in the elimination of a separate *bimah*.

Only blocks away, the Chevra Kadisha congregation, its original building having been destroyed by fire in 1920, finally found another permanent home in 1927, purchasing and renovating the former Fairmount Methodist Church Annex. This building under-went significant modification in its conversion to a synagogue. The side wings were raised to create a second level for a women's gallery.

The columns supporting the gallery are still intact and reveal a decorative detail that was no doubt part of the synagogue renovations. The lotus capital of the columns is similar to that seen in photos of the original Shearith Israel on Chenneville. The entire peaked roof was removed, probably during the process of creating sufficient height for the second level, and the peaked parapet changed to an arch following the curve of the central window. A concrete Star of David in relief marked the building as a synagogue. An adjacent building was connected by a hall to the main building and served as a residence for the *chazan sheini* (the associate cantor) who was also the building superintendent. There was a room reserved for meetings and the hall served as a daily chapel. The concrete plaque, which most certainly originally represented the tablets of the Ten Commandments, still marks the entrance of this annex. A double-sided stairway was built at the front of the building creating a new central entranceway. Despite all these very significant renovations, the interior layout of the main level was not altered to allow for the traditional central *bimah*. Thus, while in the one case a former church underwent little modification, in another building major renovations were undertaken to transform a church into a synagogue. Yet both congregations chose not to install the central *bimah*. The elimination of this traditional feature was a reflection of modernizing trends in synagogues and not a practical consideration of renovation.

In both of these synagogues a reading table was placed on the platform of the original altar space, an innovation established in the early nineteenth century by the Reform movement. The proper placement for the *bimah* had been suggested by Maimonides in the twelfth century and reinforced in the sixteenth century by Joseph Caro, the author of the legal code, the *Shulchan Aruch*, and confirmed by the commentator of the code, Moses Isserles. The *bimah* was to be near the centre of the sanctuary, in the midst of the congregation, so as not to imitate Christian placement of the pulpit next to the altar. This precept was liberally interpreted, as in Sephardic

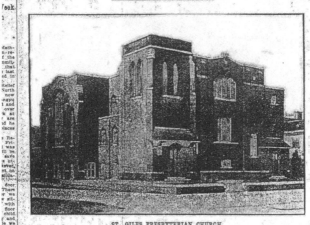

(Top) Clipping from the *Montreal Daily Witness*, April 27, 1912, announcing plans to build St. Giles Presbyterian Church on the corner of St. Joseph's Boulevard and Nelson Street, Outremont. (Bottom) The church building underwent minor renovations during its conversion to the Beth David Synagogue in 1929.

In 1927 the Chevra Kadisha congregation purchased, and dramatically renovated, the former Methodist Church Annex, 5213 Hutchison Avenue (depicted in this postcard, top).

Traces of The Past

A Portfolio by David Kaufman

1. B'nai Jacob - *172, avenue Fairmount ouest*

Built in 1918, the first synagogue in the area north of avenue Mont-Royal, the B'nai Jacob was distinguished by a sweeping arch marking the entranceway. A small portion of the original Hebrew inscription is still visible above the modern façade built to accommodate the staircase for the Collége Français.

2. Temple Solomon - *3919, rue Clark*

The Bagg Street Shul, as it is most commonly known, was built from a renovated duplex in 1921. In the late 1990s, this still-functioning synagogue was the first to benefit from a provincial grant which allowed for the repair and restoration of the exterior.

3. Temple Solomon - *3919, rue Clark*

The sanctuary, save for necessary repairs and additional lighting, has remained the same for decades. Most of the interior furnishings were obtained in 1921 from the Shaar Hashomayim when it moved from downtown to Westmount.

4. Beth Hakneseth Anshei Ukraine - *5116, rue Saint-Urbain*

Now a Ukrainian Evangelical Pentecostal church, the building was constructed as a synagogue in 1940 and still retains traces of its former use in the cornerstone tablets and on the arched plaque below the parapet where the name of the congregation, while chiseled away, can still be read.

5. Nusach Ha'ari - *100, avenue des Pins Est*

The synagogue was formed by combining several adjoining residential units. The Théâtre de Quat'Sous, which occupied the space when this photo was taken in 2000, recently demolished this building, replacing it with a glistening modern structure.

6. Shomrim Laboker - *3675, rue Saint-Dominique*

The congregation purchased a cottage in 1913 and later added this façade housing a lobby and creating an entrance and stairwell to the women's gallery. The building was sold in the 1950s to Royal Products, an egg and dairy distribution business that operated out of the premises. At the time the photo was taken, the second floor, converted from the former women's gallery, was used by the Mime Theatre.

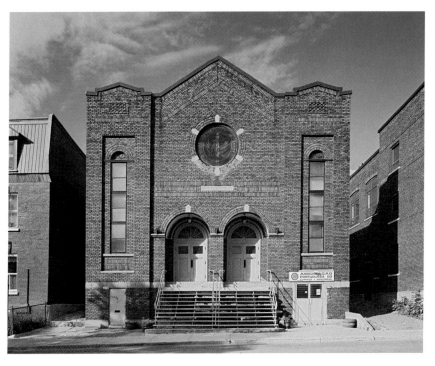

7. Beth Hamedrash Chevra Shaas - *4170, rue Saint-Urbain*

Built in 1920, this was one of the larger synagogues in the area to be purchased by subsequent groups of immigrants when the Jewish community moved to newer neighborhoods in the post-war era. The logo of the Association Portuguese fills the circular window which once housed a Star of David. The name of the synagogue remains evident on the plaque below.

8. Nusach Ha'ari, Ahavath Shalom - *5583, rue Jeanne-Mance*

In 1947, the congregation, which until then had worshipped on the ground floor of the duplex, took over the second level apartment to create a synagogue with a men's section on the main level and a women's gallery above. The prominent feature of this photo is the bimah, the reading platform, in its traditional placement central to the sanctuary and facing the aron hakodesh housing the Torah scrolls. The building was recently purchased by the Belzer Hasidic community whose members form a large part of the residents on the surrounding blocks.

9. Nusach Ha'ari, Ahavath Shalom - *5583, rue Jeanne-Mance*

A synagogue is also a house of study. On one wall of this small study corner, a Yiskor (remembrance) plaque is dedicated to the memory of deceased members. On another wall a beautiful stained glass window provides illumination for reading.

10. Poele Zedek - *7161, rue Saint-Urbain*

The building and its interior were built and crafted by the members, many of whom were carpenters and tradesmen who worked for the railway. Begun in 1910, it took at least ten years to complete. The synagogue continued to function until the late 1980s when a fire, and failed efforts to raise money for restoration, resulted in the sale to a Vietnamese religious group.

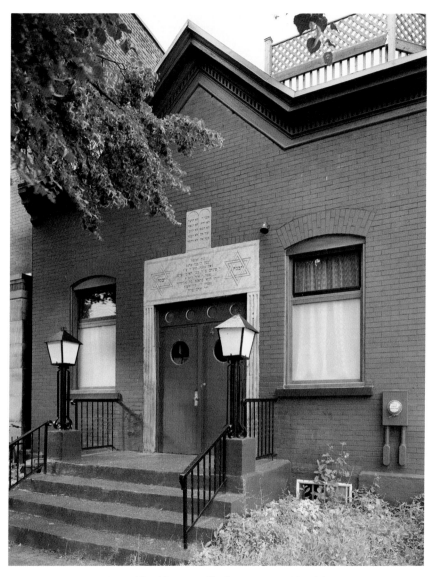

11. Yavna B'nai Parnass Shul - *4690, rue Hutchinson*

This was the second synagogue privately owned by the Parnass family. It was purchased in 1926 when a congregation of Seventh Day Adventists sought a buyer for their building who would observe the Sabbath. Services as well as a school, situated on the second floor, were offered free to the community. The building was sold in the late 90s and serves as a private residence.

12. Chevra Kadisha - *5213, rue Hutchinson*

The congregation purchased the Methodist Church in 1927. The building underwent considerable renovation in its conversion to a synagogue including the creation of a second story, which served as a women's gallery, and the addition of several arched parapets. The Ukrainian Federation removed the arches when they purchased the building in the late 1950s

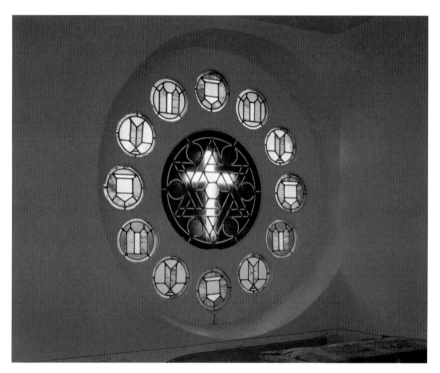

13. Beth Hakneseth Anshei Ukraine - *5116, rue Saint-Urbain*

A metal plaque with a cut out cross overlays the stained glass Star of David in what is now a Ukrainan Pentecostal church.

Montreal-born David Kaufman has had a two-track career, as a television documentary producer/director/writer and as a photographer. He worked as a news writer for CTV's *Canada AM* and in the documentary unit of the CBC's *The Journal* before he became an independent producer/director. As a photographer his major interest is architecture-based images, particularly the industrial and commercial built environment. His latest project is an ongoing exploration of the Jewish cemeteries and other historic sites in the Polish cities of Lodz, Warsaw, and Krakow. David Kaufman lives in Toronto.

and Italian synagogues where the *bimah* was located in the rear of the sanctuary.[104] However, it was the Reform movement that entirely removed the *bimah* from the floor space of the sanctuary, placing it on a platform next to the Ark. Such an arrangement diverts the focus of worship from the congregation to the clergy. It confirms the status of the rabbi and the cantor as leaders in prayer, thus removing the function from the lay prayer leaders. In traditional Judaism a rabbi, as scholar, serves the community as its authority on Jewish law. Previously his role as communal leader may have been a function of his personality but not necessarily a function of his position. The Reform movement reinvented the rabbi as preacher and leader of a synagogue congregation. The primary role of the Reform rabbi in the synagogue was to deliver edifying sermons emphasizing the moral and ethical content of Jewish tradition. Such a role required the rabbi to be physically front and centre. The elimination of the central *bimah* in the context of an Orthodox synagogue signals a similar change in the perception of the role of the rabbi. Another important physical feature distinguished the Beth David: the organ inherited from the church. Organ music was introduced by the Reform movement to create the ambiance of tranquility and spirituality experienced by worshippers in churches. The Beth David, an Orthodox congregation, did not play the organ on Shabbath and holidays, which is forbidden by Jewish law. However, the deep tones of the organ lent a desirable aura of formality to weddings held at the synagogue.[105]

Such changes in the interior of a synagogue were indeed significant indicators of modernization and a threat to the traditional rabbis. Rabbi Hirsch Cohen, a leading rabbi within the immigrant community, expressed vehement disapproval of such innovations.

> That which is occurring in your synagogue: removing the *bimah*, reversing the stance of the cantor with his face to the congregation, [installing] an organ, reminds me of the

Gemara, Shabbat 105b: "Such is the work of the evil inclination. Today it tells you do thus and tomorrow it says to you do thus until it tells you serve idolatry and you go and do it."[106]

Indeed, the Beth David congregation consciously sought to define its role as not merely a religious institution. This was evident in the use and disposition of the interior spaces. The basement of the Beth David provided space for many functions, a large and small hall and a daily chapel. These facilities, served by a fully equipped kitchen, attracted many bar mitzvahs and frequent weddings. On the occasion of its fiftieth anniversary celebration, the sisterhood is credited with having equipped and furnished appropriate facilities carrying out work "generally not undertaken by men....Thus the well equipped and comfortable position of the synagogue made the Beth David Synagogue a Jewish centre in Montreal...gaining a greater and greater importance in Jewish social life."[107]

Sonny Popliger's bar mitzvah in 1932, was not unlike today's affairs. The three hundred guests, who attended a dinner in the basement reception hall of the synagogue, included judges, lawyers, and politicians, non-Jews among them. Also like today's youth, Sonny received everything he needed to outfit a "sports-minded" young man: volley balls, soccer balls, baseballs, mitts, and hockey equipment. Such an event stands in contrast to the bar mitzvahs in the smaller *shuls* where the ceremony would be followed by a simple lunch at home in the company of close family and friends.

The long-held goal of the congregation to establish a "modern and progressive synagogue to meet the current demands and aims and to be located in a section of the city to which the members had moved"[108] was achieved through the acquisition of this building. The fiftieth anniversary in 1938 was a celebration of this accomplishment and the present status of the synagogue. It is not surprising that Rabbi Abramovitch of the Shaar Hashomayim and Rabbi Bender of the Shearith Israel were invited to bring greetings on the occasion of this historic milestone. In tribute to the Beth David, Rabbi Abramovitch notes that "loyalty to Canadian ideals" did not compromise "Jewish tradition."[109] The organizers took pride in the event as being "a holiday for the entire Jewish community" marking "a half century of Jewish activity and progress in this metropolis of the Dominion of Canada."[110] Though tribute is paid to the founders, the officers emphasized the recent achievements and drew from the past that which corresponded to their image of the present. In fact the "present generation" was even better prepared than the founders "to transmit this great Jewish heritage to generations to come."[111] The President took inspiration from the past while expressing certainty for the future.

> The Beth David congregation when first organized 50 years ago set for itself the task of introducing into the community a sense of dignity in a traditional religious service and gradually evolved an educational program to include every member of every family, particularly stressing a point of view of Jewish life which would look forward to an integrated Canadian Jewish community instead of perpetuation of distinctions based upon lands of origin.

The president's message did not convey strict adherence to convention, but appropriate change which he reported as being inherent in the congregation from its inception. A *shul* that is "modern and progressive," cannot at the same time be entirely traditional. Such words were signifiers of change, the banners of liberalizing tendencies such as the emerging Conservative movement in the States. The Beth David strove to introduce and maintain "a sense of dignity in a traditional religious service" which implied a certain decorum, emphasized in Reform Judaism, a quiet and unified manner of prayer that differed from the small *shuls* where worshippers mumbled audibly and *shockeled* visibly, each at his own pace.

The comments of the congregational rabbi were considerably more restrained than those of the lay leaders. Though the rabbi did credit the Beth David with contributing towards keeping alive a "religious sentiment" and a general "loyalty to Judaism," he bemoaned "a laxity in the observance of our rituals [and] a marked lack of knowledge of our sacred heritage…" He attributed these failings generally and not specifically to his own congregation, but suggested that the Jubilee marks not only an occasion for acknowledging "progress and achievement" but also an opportunity to address "shortcomings."[112] The author of these comments, Rabbi S. (Shia) Herschorn, is the same Yehoshua Halevi Herschorn who would extol the merits of the small *shul* in the anniversary booklet of the Anshei Ozeroff in 1943.

> The tendency in some synagogues [is] to Anglicize the *shul*, to modernize it….Instead of worship, services are held. Instead of a Jewish word from a holy text, we will hear sermons in English and book reviews…. [W]e can not create Jewishness through bible stories and sleigh rides.[113]

The words "services," "sermons," "sleigh rides," and "bible-stories" are transliterated directly from English into Yiddish, adding an obvious note of cynicism. It seems odd to parallel "bible stories," a function of religious education, with "sleigh rides," clearly a recreational activity. But neither "bible stories" nor educational programs nor even the free Sunday school, which the officers of the Beth David counted among their proudest achievements, fulfill the function of traditional learning of Torah and Talmud to which the small *shuln* had expressed a commitment. Such learning focuses on the rabbinic interpretive tradition and reasserts generations of accumulated rabbinic authority challenged by modernity. Education, it would seem, as Rabbi Herschorn wrote in tribute to the Anshei Ozeroff, is that which happens naturally in the small *shulelach*, "where a child can still see his father's eyes well with tears at a Rosh Hashanah prayer."[114]

In an invitation to his concert, Cantor Samuel Kanter is depicted in the formal attire of a concert performer in the English text and in the traditional cantor's robe in the Yiddish text.

In honour of the anniversary of his own synagogue, Rabbi Herschorn dedicated his most important remarks not to his congregants, nor to the history of the congregation, but to the historic legacy of Rumanian rabbis. He recalled the Rumanian origins of the congregation and demanded "a love and respect for Rumanian Jewry because this Jewish community radiated a strong Jewish commitment and contributed a great deal to the development of Torah [learning] and piety and religious and rabbinic literature." He praised and illustrated the innovative role of the sages of Rumanian Jewry. This topic provided him the opportunity of demonstrating his own erudition as well as his ongoing role in theological dialogue.

In light of the contrasts and comparisons between the "up-town" and "downtown" community and their respective houses of worship, the Beth David can be considered to be a "hybrid" synagogue and congregation. Located in a neighbourhood that began to approximate the uptown neighbourhoods of Westmount, it perceived itself as the focal point of the surrounding community, both religiously and socially. Its officers expressed a commitment to religious tradition at the same time as they sought to represent modernity and progress. The synagogue's interior layout abandoned aspects of the traditional synagogue. While they still identified with their Rumanian origins, they envisioned themselves as representing a mix of all Canadian Jewry, an objective which may not as yet have been accomplished. An advertisement announcing a cantorial concert exemplifies this duality of purpose and character. The concert wass billed as a "momentous" event, not only in the history of Montreal but in all of Canada. The letter appeared in both English and Yiddish. In the English version Samuel Kanter, "the most gifted tenor of the age," is shown in the formal tuxedo of a concert performer. For the Yiddish text he appears in traditional cantorial robe while holding a prayer book.

A Family *Shul*

Only one block away from the Beth David, the tiny Yavna B'nai Parnass Synagogue occupied a free standing corner building which was purchased in 1926 from the Seventh Day Adventist Church. The doorway of the plain brick exterior is flanked by shallow concrete pilasters and topped by a plaque honouring the founders and by the tablets of the Ten Commandments. The spartan interior was illuminated by bare fluorescent fixtures. A small and plain *bimah* stood in front of the *aron hakodesh* which was flanked by rows of honorary seating. A women's section was provided for in the rear of the sanctuary.

Such a description hardly fits with the designation of high-windows synagogues. However, the influence and aspirations of the founders and leaders of this synagogue exceeded the humble stature of its architecture. The Yavna Shul was the second synagogue owned and operated by the Parnass family. Pinchas Parnass established the first family *shul* in 1910, the Kerem Israel, located in the second area of settlement. As both the community and the family moved north and west, the family sought an additional location which eventually replaced the original *shul*. The Yavna Shul was purchased by Pinchas for his wife Raizel in honour of their twenty-fifth wedding anniversary. Raizel had long wished to establish a family synagogue in honour and in memory of her father who had had his own *shul* in Russia. This was not an uncommon practice Europe, but the Parnass family was the only one to have established a privately owned *shul* in Montreal. When the Seventh Day Adventists advertised for purchasers who observed the Sabbath, the Parnass family took advantage of the opportunity and Raizel became the patroness of her own *shul*.

The Yavna shul was the second synagogue owned and operated by the Parnass family. From left to right: Abraham, Boris, Raizel, Motel, Pinchas (Paul), Harry, Sara, and Joseph.

The preamble to the synagogue's constitution, an acrostic poem in the original Hebrew spelling the name "Raizel" vertically, confirmed her status as benefactor and expressed the mission and the legacy that she bequeathed to her husband, her four sons, and one daughter.

> Firstly the Yavna synagogue was founded
> In the coming days honest words will be engraved
> In the memory of the last generation, children and
>   children of children
> Will receive these things upon themselves and their seed
> This holy place will be known as a house of worship
> Joy and prayer will be carried to he who dwells on high.
> This house, dedicated by a kosher and modest woman
> In pure generosity, sanctified to the heavens
> Her words [of dedication] have acquired [the synagogue]
>   for heavenly [purposes], a responsibility bequeathed to
>   coming generations.[115]

The constitution spelled out a clear mission for the trustees and their descendants: the property could never be used for anything other than a *shul* and it could never be placed in jeopardy as security for a loan. As in the family's earlier *shul*, the second floor was to house a free Talmud Torah school for children and High Holiday services were open to anyone in the community without the need to purchase seats. The congregation was to follow a strict Orthodox tradition using, as was not uncommon in smaller congregations, the *Nusach Sepharad*, the Sephardic ritual, and no reforms could be brought into the practices of the *shul*. Pinchas and Raizel's granddaughter states that the family originated from Spain and that they maintained the Spanish ritual throughout their centuries-long sojourn in Russia. Notwithstanding the particularity of the Parnass family history, the *Nusach Sepharad* was adopted by the Hasidim of Eastern Europe. Many smaller congregations in Montreal continued to use this ritual version even in the absence of a fully articulated Hasidic social setting or the leadership of a Hasidic *rebbe*.

If one measures the extent of her gift not only as a small brick building and plot of land but as a legacy of devotion and commitment to family, tradition, and community, Raizel's bequest was an enduring one. The family had gained both economic and community prominence and their influence and energy extended well beyond the walls of their tiny *shul*. Raizel and Pinchas's eldest son was particularly notable. Abraham Parnass was a founder and active leader in many community organizations with a special commitment to Jewish education. He was a founder and supporter of schools with diverse ideologies: J. Peretz School, Jewish People's School, and the Rabbinical College of Tomchei Timimim Lubavitch. He was a co-founder of the Jewish Public Library and president of Jewish Community Services, was involved in the Jewish Convalescent Home, and the Jewish National Workers, Alliance (which had been established by his parents in 1910). He also served as a delegate to the first Canadian Jewish Congress in 1919.

Nan Wiseman, Abraham's granddaughter, relates a story of Abraham's quiet generosity on the occasion of his fiftieth wedding anniversary. Nan agreed to help him out by acting as his driver for the day and escorted him to fifty different Jewish educational institutions where he left a gift of fifty dollars. "At each place," she recalls, "he got a personal welcome, with hugs and kisses from the secretary in the office to the rabbi of the school." But his greatest passion was reserved for the Jewish People's School. "My grandfather was in the school every single day. When he died, the school actually took over his whole funeral. There was a procession past the school and a large banner photograph was hung above the building."

Joseph Parnass, the youngest brother, lived until the age of one hundred and five and carried on both the tradition of family benefactor and community activist. His daughter Helen Constantine lauded her father as "the mainstay of the family" who invested both emotion-ally and financially in the family's welfare. Emulating the tradition of the highest level of *tzedakah*, his donations were anonymous and made in honour of his parents. He was one of the founders of Canadian Jewish Congress and a founding member of the Rabbin-ical College of Canada.

The Parnass family, having immigrated to Montreal in 1903 and now established after twenty to thirty years, exhibited concerns beyond those of the immediate welfare of immigrants. The synagogue was both the focal point and the extension of their aspirations to foster a fully developed community. They were as equally willing to support the Lubavitch Yeshiva as they were committed to the Labour-Zionist-oriented Jewish People's School. They helped establish the Jewish National Workers' Alliance even while they were themselves prominent merchants. The communal institutions which they founded and supported were not replicas or replacements for those which they had left behind in Europe. These institutions served the diverse social, cultural, political, and educational needs of developing Montreal Jewry.

The Synagogue as Community Centre

The idea of the synagogue centre has been attributed to Mordecai Kaplan, the founder of the Reconstructionist movement. Practic-ally, the efforts of the Reform movement both pre-dated and implemented his ideas, which came to be adopted by both Conservative and Orthodox rabbis who sought to reconcile the tensions between Judaism and the social aspiration of modern Jews. The synagogue centre movement, fully conceived in several large congregations in the United States in the early part of the century and into the twenties, attempted to converge all aspects of Jewish life into a single facility which might have included a library, a gymnasium, and a school, multiple meeting rooms, and multi-function halls, even swimming pools. Following World War II, the centre movement spread to the suburbs where decentralized Jewish communities took advantage of larger plots of land to create new centres of activity which merged religious with social functions.

As David Kaufman has summarized in his study, *Shul with a Pool*, the success of the synagogue centre was dependent less on the ideologies of the rabbinic elite than upon the energies of the laity. It was dependent on three converging factors: aspirations of the second generation, their solid middle-class status, and the physical opportunities in new neighbourhoods. Kaufman concludes that "the synagogue centre is the first synagogue type without precedent in the European past. It is originally and quintessentially American."[116]

The Adath Israel congregation was among the first in Montreal to conceive of itself as a synagogue and community centre. The congregation was incorporated in 1938 under the name of the "Adath Israel Congregation and Community Centre of Outremont." The architect's preliminary plans for the synagogue were labelled "Outremont Jewish Community Centre." This is the only synagogue in the four consecutive areas of settlement that is not located within close proximity to several other synagogues. It was located in the heart of Outremont, a free-standing building, in an entirely residential community. The lot was sufficiently large to accommodate future expansion. Built in 1940, its congregants and leaders certainly included a large proportion of second generation Canadians. The anniversary publication indicates no country or place of origin of its founders. The members were probably those residing in this middle to upper-middle-class neighbourhood. Established in 1930, and initially utilizing a rented hall several blocks away, this is the only one of the *shuln*, or larger synagogues, that did not originate in the first area of settlement.

Despite the self-definition as a community centre, one searches in vain for the pool within this *shul* in the architectural drawings. The YMHA, just over two kilometres away, probably adequately served the recreational needs of the community. The plans allow for little more of the multi-functional spaces than were already available in the other large synagogues. The lower level contains a multi-purpose auditorium and kitchen, as well as an apartment for the caretaker and a meeting room for the ladies'

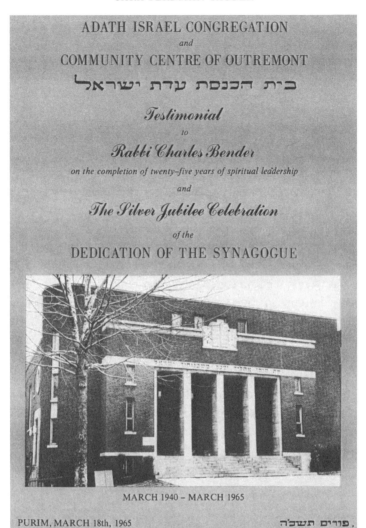

ADATH ISRAEL CONGREGATION
and
COMMUNITY CENTRE OF OUTREMONT

בית הכנסת עדת ישראל

Testimonial
to
Rabbi Charles Bender
on the completion of twenty-five years of spiritual leadership

and

The Silver Jubilee Celebration

of the

DEDICATION OF THE SYNAGOGUE

MARCH 1940 – MARCH 1965

PURIM, MARCH 18th, 1965   פורים תשכ״ה,

Anniversary program of the Adath Israel Congregation and
Community Centre, Outremont, March 18, 1965.

108

auxiliary. The sanctuary level also has a chapel and office with additional offices above including a rabbi's study and library. The congregation's primary definition of "community centre" then would seem to focus on the establishment of a school. The original elementary school facilities were in the basement and it was, according to the anniversary publication, not only the first congregational day school in Montreal, but also only the second in all of North America. By 1947 a school building was constructed in the adjacent rear lot which was extended in 1952 to accommodate Montreal's first Jewish high school day school.[117]

While not providing space for all the functions that the idea of synagogue centre implies, the building does mark a significant transition in Montreal synagogue architecture from traditional to modern, or more specifically, from the historic eclecticism of the nineteenth century and the early twentieth century to modernism. Though the brick building was thoroughly traditional in terms of building materials and techniques, its design was influenced by the geometric simplicity of volume and form as exemplified by the Bauhaus movement. Bauhaus-inspired architecture was, at the time, becoming the predominant buiding style in the emerging new city of Tel Aviv. It is both interesting, and exceedingly rare, that we have an early non-built architectural proposal, that of architect H.W. Davis. Though it appears to be influenced by modernism in its volumetric simplicity, verticality of arched windows, and minimal ornamentation, the overall impression is still in keeping with traditional religious architecture in Montreal in which such details as the brickwork and the series of arches punctuating the roof line are prominent. The plan which was ultimately chosen was designed by Jewish architects, Eliasoph and Greenspoon. Its shape is entirely rectilinear, broken only by a semi-cylinder on the northwest corner which houses a stairwell. The arched fenestration, which typically characterized the synagogues of Montreal, is replaced by narrow rectangles topped with circular clerestory windows. The entranceway, as well, is neither peaked nor arched but is articulated as a prominent rectangle divided into four bays by three square pillars devoid of any ornamentation. The building is marked as a synagogue by a Hebrew inscription above the entrance topped by the tablets of the Ten Commandments which are flanked by a lion and an eagle. This is the only such iconographic symbol on a synagogue in Montreal. It has been suggested that it represents the quotation from *Pirkeh Avoth* (Ethics of the Fathers): Devotion to God should be as "the speed of an antelope, the strength of a lion, the perseverance of a leopard, (and) the swiftness of an eagle."[118]

The interior is replete with iconographic and custom details of which the stained glass is the most important. Both the style and the content of the visual details are modern and do not rely on traditional prototypes. Aside from the usual *magen david*, stylized elements suggest staffs of wheat or biblical species of plants and indicate a renewed connection to "the land" and agriculture. The chapel features leaded windows whose gridwork forms multiple *magen davids*. The light fixtures in the sanctuary, incised with *magen davids*, are not unusual. The attention to iconographic detail extends even to the door knobs which are embossed with a *magen david* superimposed on a seven-branched *menorah*.

The design of the *aron hakodesh* is a departure from the traditional "temple" form of peaked pediment flanked by columns. References to oriental influences are still evident, though in a modernized form, in the prominent vaulted niche which forms the space housing the Ark, especially in the intricate latticework above the Ark reminiscent of Islamic decorative elements.

In the layout of the interior we still find the traditional central *bimah* in this Modern Orthodox synagogue. But the overall division of space represented a first in the context of these "immigrant synagogues." As in the earlier Shaar Hashomayim in Westmount, the women's galleries were abandoned in favour of a women's section which is only a few steps up from the central men's section. There were no railings or curtains obstructing the women's view.

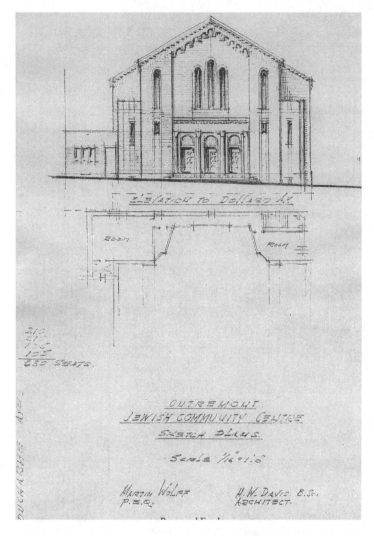

Although influenced by modernism, architect H.W. Davis's proposed plan for Adath Israel, which was never built, reflected a traditional religious sensibility.

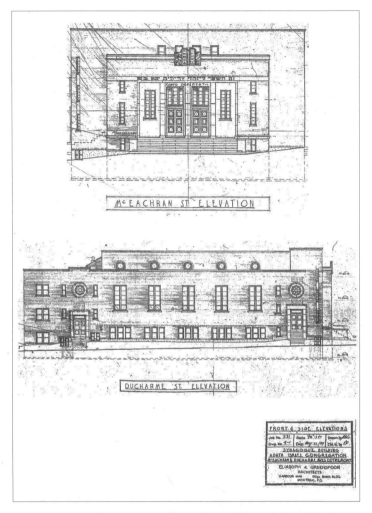

Built in 1940, the Adath Israel's modern building, designed by the architectural firm Eliasoph & Greenspoon, included a multi-purpose auditorium below the sanctuary, and the later addition of Montreal's first Jewish day school.

Both the proximity of the women and the central *bimah* create a sense of spatial intimacy that is consistent with the notion of communality.

The first indication of a modernist approach to synagogue architecture appeared as early as 1903 in the conceptual drawings for a competition for design of a synagogue in Trieste, Austro-Hungary. But actual construction of synagogues in a modern idiom in Europe did not take place until the late twenties and thirties. It was only with the arrival of Jewish architects fleeing Nazi Europe that modern designs began to be considered for synagogues in the Unites States.[119] The Adath Israel Synagogue, built in 1940, may well have an architectural significance beyond the context of Montreal alone.

If the space itself does not seem to have provided for a diversity of functions, the organizational structure of the Adath Israel indicates that there was considerable opportunity for community involvement. A men's club, sisterhood, choir, and junior congregation, or in this case, the young people's service club, were part of the structure of many synagogues. The day school also provided opportunities for participation in a home and school association. But the boys' and girls' scout troops established in 1940 and 1941 as congregational groups, had, of course, nothing to do with Judaism and everything to do with integration into the Canadian social milieu. On a wall of the synagogue one more item indicates that by 1945 this congregation was perhaps more Canadian than it was Eastern European. An honour roll listed the names of eighty-nine members who had served in the Canadian armed forces during World War II.

The four congregations bordering on and in Outremont represented a maturing immigrant community whose focus was no longer on what was left behind but on building a future that was both Jewish and Canadian. Accolades in the Beth David anniversary publication laud a "modern and progressive" congregation

Adath Israel. (Top) Wedding, 1980, and (bottom), a high school graduation, year unknown.

whose values represent a "loyalty to Canadian ideals...in keeping with Jewish tradition." In retrospect, even the founders, "men of light and learning," were seen as "Jewish Cana-dians in the best sense of the term." After fifty years of existence, the leadership consciously strove to foster "a point of view of Jewish life which would look forward to an integrated Canadian Jewish community instead of perpetuation of distinctions based upon lands of origin." The purchase of "this beautiful edifice" in a then new part of town allowed the Beth David to become "a Jewish centre in Montreal...gaining greater and greater importance in Jewish social life."

The contrast between the tiny Parnass Shul and the imposing Beth David is striking. In its modest and practical approach to furnishing its *shul*, the Parnass Shul was identical to the *shulelach* of the second and third areas. But this is not a *landsmanshaft shul*. The generosity which the Parnass family exhibited in helping a neighbourhood through this synagogue was extended, with its vision of establishing diversifed institutions serving Montreal's Jewish community.

The Adath Israel represents, physically and conceptually, a transition between old and new. It was located on the very edge of the last area of concentration of the immigrant community; its style is more modern than any previously built synagogue in Montreal; and it had adopted a synagogue model, the synagogue centre, which though not yet fully conceived, was based on American rather than European prototypes.

Shuln and *Shulelach*

THE SIZE OF THE BUILDING has emerged as a major theme throughout this story of immigrant synagogues in Montreal. It is an indi-
cator of identity and as a measure of the aspirations of the congregations. It is obvious that a large building of any type would visually
communicate confidence and permanence. In the context of an
immigrant community a large institutional building is a sign of
integration, of transfer of identity from the mother country to the
adopted home. The presence of small communal buildings is,
perhaps, not only a measure of lack of means but a lack of desire,
indicating instead that the congregations valued intimacy and
resisted change. This interpretation is strengthened by comparison
with the development of synagogues in Europe in the modern
era. Traces of historic tension and even conflict between assimilationists and traditionalists in the modernizing Jewish communities of Europe might well be perceived in the contrast between
shul and *shulechel* in the immigrant community of Montreal. But
finally, the voices recorded in oral histories have coloured such
perception with yet another layer of complexity.

Throughout the nineteenth century, the era of emancipation,
the very presence of monumental synagogues redefined Jewish
presence in the cityscape, confirming a new Jewish identity as
citizen of the nation of residence and establishing the synagogue,
as Hayoun and Jarrase wrote, "as the very symbol of the emancipation." [120] They noted the words of Rabbi Isaac Levy on the occasion of the inauguration of a synagogue in 1861 in Switzerland.

Every time that one of our old synagogues disappears in order to make room for a larger and more beautiful one, it is the dark image of the past that fades in order that we can perceive the radiant face of modern civilization.[121]

The history of many of the synagogues of Europe, erected in this spirit of optimism during the era of Emancipation, came to an end in the years between 1938 and 1945. At the twenty-fifth anniversary of the Anshei Ozeroff in 1943, the president's dedicatory remarks highlight a poignant contrast and a different reality:

In the time when the Jewish folk, saturated with sorrow over the tragedy of the Jews of Europe, we, the Beth Haknesseth Anshei Ozeroff, are marking the twenty-fifth anniversary and the dedication of our building to prove to our enemies that Jewry will not go under. There, synagogues are destroyed, but here, we are fortunate to be able to build synagogues.[119]

As the immigrant community of Montreal matured, it too sought to build large, even monumental and opulent synagogues that asserted a presence. The Beth Yehuda was opened with "splendour and with glory," having spared no expenses in erecting "such a fine building that is the pride of all Montreal Jews." The B'nai Jacob confidently constructed the first synagogue in a new neighbourhood marking its façade with a majestic arch and inscribed Star of David. The aspiration of the Beth David to be a "modern and progressive" congregation, "a Jewish centre in Montreal," was reflected in its well-equipped synagogue whose reception facilities were designed to serve the social needs of the community. Ironically, its congregational rabbi, Rabbi Yehoshua Herschorn, decried such efforts, criticizing "the mistake that was made through grand buildings, and beautiful walls and carpets..." These are "errors only to be found in the large synagogues" while the "small *shulelach* maintain the true traditional Judaism without deviation and without modernizations."

While the contrast between *shul* and *shulechel* reflects a distinction in orientation, and perhaps aspiration, it does not suggest the same level of conflict as the confrontation between the Maskilim of Galicia and the Hasidic *minyamim* or the *consistoire* of Paris and the Eastern European immigrant congregations where assimilationists sought governmental injunctions against the traditionalists. The social, cultural, and religious relations within the immigrant community of Montreal were probably far less polarized. Generally, those who chose to leave the Old World for the New were not among the most traditional; the courage required to cross an ocean to establish a new life already implies considerable willingness to change and to challenge tradition. Even the small synagogues, despite the claims of their leaders, were not representative of a particularly pious community. The *landsmanshaft shul* was by definition a consequence of the immigrant experience rather than a replica of the tradition-bound small synagogues of Europe. This was a social as well as religious hub for family and friends from the same area, city, or town. Yet while some immigrants remained committed to their particular *schulechel*, others, especially over the course of time, would attend the one which was most convenient, offered the best price for holiday tickets, featured a talented cantor, or provided the most suitable space for marking a wedding or a bar mitzvah.

The recollections of ordinary people who used these synagogues and lived in these neighbourhoods reveal a relationship to religion and between religious and secular ideologies that was far less polarized than one might expect. Lawrence Popliger attended the Beth David with his parents, but, contrary to orthodox practice, took the trolley on *Shabbos* to be with his grandfather at the more traditional Adath Yeshurun. Abraham Parnass, the eldest son of the founders of the family *shul* whose constitution forbade the introduction of any ritual reforms, supported the Lubavitch Yeshiva but was particularly devoted to the Labour-Zionist-oriented Jewish People's School. Joseph Rapoport, the son of a wealthy capitalist, sang in the choir of the B'nai Jacob but was also a member of the mandolin orchestra at the nearby Workmen's Circle (the cultural and educational arm of the Bund, the Polish Jewish socialist move-ment) and participated in social events at the Young Communist League. Ben Zion Dalfen came from a very observant family who attended the Tallner Beit Hamidrash Centre run by a Hasidic rabbi. Yet, he too visited the Centre for the Communist Party, situated just around the corner, in the quest for a good ping-pong game.

It is possible that the particular density of this neighbourhood, which was not so crowded as to be alienating while being populated enough to be ideologically diverse, may have accounted for a breaking down of barriers. That this might be a confluence of factors unique to Montreal would certainly be an interesting subject for further study. Over the course of the first half of the twentieth century, Jews from different countries, cities and towns, religious Jews and secular Jews, union leaders and owners of businesses, played together at the YMHA and listened to the same cultural programs at the Jewish Public Library. While the little *shulelach* welcomed their *landsleit* and provided a haven of familiarity, the neighbourhood forged a new identity—the Montreal Jewish community.

Where Are They Now?

DURING THE WAR YEARS, and immediately following, the community had begun moving west into newer neighbourhoods and by the late fifties and sixties into the post-war suburbs. The synagogues of Plateau Mont-Royal and Outremont absorbed the arriving Holocaust survivors, among them various ultra-Orthodox sects. It is the *Haredi* community who remain visible along the streets east and west of Park Avenue today. As the original congregations began to migrate, the Hasidim took over some of the *shtibels*. The small and large synagogues, however, were sold beginning in the late fifties and continuing into the late eighties, to subsequent groups of immigrants as houses of worship, assembly, or community centres. Small prayer rooms in triplexes and duplexes and in business premises have reverted to residential and commercial use. While about fifteen Jewish houses of worship can still be counted in these neighbourhoods, only one represents the original pre-World War II congregation.

A handful of regular members continue to attend Temple Solomon—the Bagg Street Shul—and until its purchase by the Belzer Hasidic community in 2007, the Nusach Ha'ari on Jeanne-Mance Street. Some of the older congregants still live in the surrounding streets. Some younger worshippers have rediscovered the charms of the area and live in this newly fashionable district. But others find their way there from more remote parts of the city, perhaps seeking a greater sense of intimacy and authenticity which has been lost in the large, modern, "uptown" synagogues. Temple Solomon has in the last few years benefited from a provincial government grant for restoration and renovation in recognition of its heritage status.[122] But most of all, the longevity of these buildings is due, in large part, to the caretakers Joe Brick and Max Rothman, who guarded the keys and continued to look after their *shuls*. Both Joe and Max have passed on but I dedicate these final words to their memory. They saw to it that the windows were repaired, the floors mopped now and then, occasionally arranged for *kiddish* after services and opened the door to visitors exploring the traces of the past.

While only physical traces of Montreal's Jewish religious heritage remain in the old neighbourhoods, the legacy of the congregations remains vibrant and ever-changing. In the post-war years, most of the congregations amalgamated and built new buildings in new communities. The names of their amalgamated congregations form lengthy inscriptions on the exteriors of the new buildings, testaments to the desire to maintain a connection to their early histories. The names of Shomrim Laboker, Shaare Tefilah, Beth Yehuda, Tifereth Israel, Beth Hamedrash Hagadol (with Tifereth Joseph naming their daily chapel) are written on the side of a synagogue built in the fifties, recalling synagogues large and small which once marked the streets of the early immigrants. Congregation Chevra Shaas Adath Yeshurun Hadrath Kodesh Shevet Achim Chaverim Kol Israel d'Bet Avraham represents an amalgamation of five former "downtown" congregations. After nearly a century of association with its Eastern European immigrant roots, this amalgamated congregation merged in 2005 with the oldest congregation in Canada, the Shearith Israel, now known as the Spanish and Portuguese Congregation. Zichron Kedoshim is an affiliation of Anshei Ukraina, Beth Matesyohu, Beth Moishe, and Beth Israel and Samuel, all congregations from the old neighbourhoods. In fact, as the congregations left their original synagogues, moving into Snowdon, Côte St. Luc, and Hampstead, they amalgamated with each other and remained Orthodox. The pattern of early synagogue formation in neighbourhoods of Eastern

Some amalgamated congregations.

European Jewish immigrants is probably similar to others in urban centres in Canada and the United States, but their unanimous continued affiliation with orthodoxy is unique to Montreal. While this is one of the most interesting aspects to arise in the course of investigation, the explanations remain a matter of further inquiry and material for another story.

The back of the B'nai Jacob Synagogue as seen from the lane.
In the rear of many buildings that once housed synagogues, tracings in
the brick silently recall the circular stained-glass windows that once
illuminated the space above the Torah Ark.

]

Endnotes

PREFACE
1 CJCNA/synagogues ZG/B'nai Jacob, B.G. Sack, "Our Old Orthodox Synagogues," *Keneder Adler*, October 19, 1958.

INTRODUCTION AND ALL CHAPTERS
1 From *Master of Prayer*, quoted by Calvin Goldscheider and Alan S. Zuckerman. *The Transformation of the Jews* (University of Chicago Press, Chicago and London, 1984) p. 32.

2 Gerald Wolfe. Synagogues of the Lower Eastside of New York (Washington Mews Books, Division of NYU Press, New York, 1978) p.28.

3 Joseph Guttman. *No Graven Images-Studies in Art and the Hebrew* Bible (KTAV Publishing House Inc., New York, 1971) p. XVI.

4 David Biale. *Cultures of the Jews* (Schocken Books, New York, 2002) p.xvii.

5 John Gloag. *The Architectural Interpretation of History* (St. Martin's Press, New York, 1975) p.1 and p.22.

6 Richard I. Cohen. *Jewish Icons: Art and Society in Modern Europe* (University of California Press, Berkeley, Los Angeles, London, 1998) p.8.

7 Ibid., p.2.

8 Ibid., Chapter 3, "Rabbi as Icon," pp.115-153.

9 Ibid., p.141.

10 "The 60s: The Global Village" at the Montreal Museum of Fine Arts, fall 2003-winter 2004.

"Warhol's Garbage" by Armand Pierre Fernandez, 1969.

11 Israel Medres. *Montreal of Yesterday*. translated from the Yiddish by Vivian Felsen (Véhicule Press, Montreal) pp.21-22. Original publication (Keneder Adler Press, Montreal, 1947).

Israel Medres immigrated to Montreal from Russia in 1910. He became a reporter for the Keneder Adler and a chronicler of the early Jewish community.

12 Louis Rosenberg. "Canadian Jewish Population Studies No. 2, The Jewish Population of Canada, A Statistical Study from 851-1941." p. 17. Reprinted from the *American Jewish Year Book*, Vol. 48, 1946-47.

13 Recollection of Maxwell Goldstein who at age 19 attended the first organizing meeting on August 24, 1882 together with his father and brothers. "Temple Emanu-El Jubillee Celebration, 1932" p.8.

14 Shearith Israel was located on Chenneville at Lagauchetiere. The Corporation of English German and Polish Jews was at 41 St. Constant, later Cadieux and now de Bullion. The first two rented facilities of Temple Emanu-El were in the "uptown" area both around St. Catherine and Drummond.

15 The Montifiore Club was established in 1880 as an elite Jewish secular, social club providing literary and dramatic programs. The Elmridge Country Club was established as a Jewish golf club in 1925.

16 CJCNA/synagogues ZG/Shearith Israel/ "One Hundred and Fiftieth Anniversary of the Spanish and Portuguese Jews of Montreal," 1918, p.17.

17 Ibid. p.39.

18 Ibid. p.51.

19 Rachel Witnitzer. "The Egyptian Synagogue Revival." Gutman. *The Synagogue* (Ktav, New York, 1975).

20 Samuel Gruber. *The American Synagogue* (Rizzolli, New York, 2003) p.29.

21 Krzysztof Stephanski, quoted by Jacek Walicki. *Synagogues and Prayer Houses of Lodz*. Translation by Guy Russel Torr. (DRUK, Lodz, 2000) p.25.

22 The development of synagogue styles (late 18th-19th centuries) is discussed in the following sources:

Dominique Jarrassé and Maurice-Ruben Hayoun, *Synagogues* (Societé Nouvelle Adam Biro, Paris, 2001, English translation, Vilo International, Paris, 2001) pp.145-166.

Carol Herselle Krinsky. *The Synagogues of Europe* (Dover Publications, Mineola, New York, 1985) pp.59-104.

23 Krinksy. pp. 313-315.

24 Paul Trepannier and Richard Dubé. *Montréal, Une Adventure Urbaine* (Pointe-à-Callière Museum, Montréal, 2000) "...les synagogues ont été a Montréal les premiers edifies religieux a adopter un vocabulaire oriental." p. 167.

25 Rabbi Harry Stern. "A Word of Greeting," CJCNA/synagogues ZG/Temple Emanu-El, "Fiftieth Anniversary, 1882-1931, Congregation Emanu-El," p.2.

26 Zelda Landsman. CJCNA/synagogues ZG/Temple Emanu-El, "Temple Emanuel, the First 78 years," 1970.

27 Jarrassé. pp. 171-202 and Krinsky. Passim.

28 "Dedication Service: A Historical Sketch, September 17, 1922," CJCNA/synagogue/Shaar Hashomayim, pp.13-14.

29 Ibid.

30 Based on statistics provided by Louis Rosenberg. "Changes in the Geographical Distribution of the Jewish Population of Montreal in the Decennial Periods from 1901 to 1911." (Bureau of social and Ecomonic Research, Candian Jewish Congress, Montreal, 1966), p.5.

31 Beth Yehuda anniversary booklet of 1940. History written by Gidaliahu Michalovsky, a former president, gathered from the archives of the synagogue and from recollections of older members. The text was translated from the Yiddish by Sara Tauben.

32 *The Jewish Times*, Special Number, Dec.11, 1899, "History of the Jewish Communal Bodies of Montreal," p.19.

33 The newspaper clipping does not indicate the name of the newspaper. CJCNA/synagogues ZG/ Chevra Kadisha.

34 Ibid. *The Jewish Times*, Special Number, p. 15.

35 B.G. Sack. "A Shul that Reminds us of the Pioneers of Yesterday: Our Own B'nai Jacob Shul, a Chapter of the Jewish Past." *Keneder Adler*. September 9, 1951 Translated from the Yiddish by Sara Tauben. CJCNA/synagogue ZG/ B'nai Jacob. B.G. Sack was a columnist for the *Keneder Adler*. This article is one in a series about Montreal's old synagogues. Sack is recognized as the first historian of the Canadian Jewish community.

36 Bernard Figler. "The Story of Two Congregations-Chevra Kadisha and Benai Jacob." CJCNA/synagogue ZG/Chevra Kadisha.

37 Judith Seidel, "The Development and Social Adjustment of the Jewish Community in Montreal." Master's thesis, Department of Sociology, McGill University, 1939, pp-63-64.

38 Ibid. pp. 108-109.

39 Isadore Albin, taped interview.

40 Edward Wolkove, taped interview.

41 Louis Rosenberg. "The Jewish Population of Canada–A Statistical Summary," Reprinted from the American Jewish Yearbook, Vo. 48, 1946-47 containing statistical supplement for period 1951-54. Rosenberg qualifies the term "mother tongue as being problematic and described by the census bureau in different ways in various years

ranging from the language most commonly spoken at home to the language learned in childhood but perhaps no longer even understood. Nevertheless, based on my own experience interviewing former former residents of these neighborhoods, the vast majority (80%) indicated Yiddish as the language spoken at home despite the fact that large majority (over 80%?) of my interviewees were Canadian born.

42 Based on the age of interviewees who recounted this memory, this might have been a custom during the 30s, 40s, and 50s.

43 Rosenberg. "The Jewish Population of Canada, 1850-1943", p.17.

44 The number of congregations may have been higher. My estimate of 31 congregations corresponds with the UdM study, however, Louis Rosenberg notes that "39 congregations in Montreal and Outremont in 1941 were concentrated in an area with in one mile radius of the corner of Fairmount and Hutchinson Streets." Outside of this area, he lists Shaar Hashomayim, Temple Emanu-El, and Shaar Zion. Shearith Israel on Stanley probably falls within the 1 mile radius. The three synagogues in the Papineau area are not included in his count as well as perhaps four other smaller congregations which would fall outside of his one mile radius. If we combine his figures with mine, and adjust for the geographic areas as defined in this study, there might have been a total of 49 congregations in Montreal with 38 in the area of greatest concentration.

45 Wolfe. *The Synagogues of New York's Lower East Side,* p.31.

46 Based on the respondents of my study, only 8.3% of the fathers and 4.7% of the sons attended synagogue daily.

47 Taped interview, 2000.

48 *Keneder Adler,* "Our Synagogues," Sept. 7, 1934, p.8. Translated from the Yiddish by Sara Tauben.

49 Ira Robinson. "A letter from the Sabbath Queen: Rabbi Yudel Rosenberg Addresses Montreal Jewry." *An Everyday Miracle: Yiddish Culture in Montreal.* (Véhicule Press, Montreal, 1990) p. 111.

50 T   aped interview, April 6, 2000

51 B.G. Sack. "Sixty years of existence of a shul," sixtieth anniversary publication of 1936. Translated by Sara Tauben.

52 Israel Medres. *Montreal of Yesterday.,* Keneder Adler Press, Montreal, 1947, p.28 Translated from the Yiddish by Sara Tauben.

53 Rabbi Solomon Frank. *Two Centuries in the Life of a Synagogue*

(history of Shearith Israel) p. 81.

54 Ibid. Medres. 'Montreal of Yesterday," p.22.

55 Sara Jacobs, taped interview, January 25, 2000.

56 Cantor Shimshon Hamerman, in describing the amalgamated congregations of today's Tifereth Beth David Jerusalem, indicates this designated seating for *kohanim* with regards to the Beth Itzhak, synagogue bulletin, July-August, 1980.

57 Krinsky. p.387.

58 The possible existence of women's galleries in medieval Spanish synagogues is mentioned in the following sources:

Krinsky. pp 333, 335.

Felipe Torroba and Bernaldo de Quiros. *The Spanish Jews,* (Libros Certeza) p. 72, 80.

59 Krinsky. comments on women's galleries: pp.28-31, 51-2, 299, 363.

60 Taped interviews: Harvey Berger, January 25, 2001; Irving Halperin, May 3, 2001, Lawrence Popliger, September 6, 2000.

61 Bernard Figler. *Canadian Jewish Profiles; Rabbi Dr. Herman Abramowitz, Lazarus Cohen, Lyon Cohen,* Ottawa, 1968.

62 Hirsch Wolofsky. *Journey of My Life* (The Eagle Publishing Co. Ltd., Montreal, 1945) p. 80. Wolofsy was founder of the Canader Adler and vice-president of the Adath Yeshurun at the time of the dedication.

63 Thomas Hubka, "The Gwozdziec-Chodorow Group of Wooden Synagogues." *"Polin"* vol. II, edited by Anthony Polansky (Littman Library of Jewish Civilization, 1998) pp141-182.

64 Tzvi Langerman. "Some Astrological Themes in the Thought of Abraham Ibn Ezra." In *Rabbi Ibn Ezra.* edited by Issador Twersky and Jay M. Harris (Harvard UP, 1993) p. 50.

65 Matityahu Glazerman. *Above the Zodiac, Astrology in Jewish Thought* (Aronson, Inc., Nothvale, New Jersey, 1997).

66 According to Joe Brick, the caretaker of the synagogue.

67 B.G. Sack. "Our Old Orthodox Shuls." *Keneder Adler,* October 19, 1958, p. 4 .

68 Gidalyahu Michalovsky. "Beth Yehuda 50th Anniversary." 1940 Translated from the Yiddish by Sara Tauben.

69 Ibid.

70 Yehoshua Halevi Herschorn. "In Honour of the 25th Anniversay of a Small Shul: The Anshei Ozeroff." Printed in

"Congregation Anshei Ozeroff Silver Jubilee and Opening of Our Newly Erected Synagogue, 1918-1934, 5244 St. Urbain Street." (From the private collection of Rachel Birenbaum and Jean Zwirek, Montreal.) Translated from the Yiddish by Sara Tauben.

71 Souvenir book honouring Rabbi Hirsch Cohen, 1940, translated from the Yiddish by Sara Tauben. CJCNA/VJC collection series ZB/ Hirsch Cohen.

72 Percy Tannenbaum, based on notes of phone conversation, 2001.

73 Yolette Mendelson, based on taped interview, May 31, 2001.

74 Olive Brumer, based on taped interview, July 19, 2000.

75 S. Birenbaum, "A Survey of Seventeen Years of Involvement in the Shul" *Congregation Anshei Ozeroff Silver Jubilee and Opening of Our Newly Erected Synagogue, 1918-1943, 5244 St. Urbain Street.* From the private collection of Rachel Birenbaum and Jean Zwirek. Yiddish texts translated by Sara Tauben.

76 Souvenir booklet honouring Rabbi Hirsch Cohen, author unknown, translated from the Yiddish by Sara Tauben.

77 Hielel Adler. *Memories of Ozarow, A Little Jewish Town That Was.* translated from French by William Fraiberg (published in 1997 by William Fraiberg and congregation Anshei Ozeroff, Montreal).

78 The minute book of the Anshei Ozeroff is in the private collection of the daughter, Jean Zwirek and widow, Rachel Birenbaum of the former secretary, Shlomo (Sam) Birenbaum. They preserved it as a memento to Sam who passed away unexpectedly upon returning from a meeting planning the 25th anniversary. The minutes were translated from the Yiddish by Sara Tauben and Rochelle Ferdman.

79 Ibid. *Anshei Ozeroff,* R.I.K. Goldblum, executive director of Kerem Kayemet, Canada.

80 Ibid. *Anshei Ozeroff,* Rabbi Yehoshua Halevi Herschorn, "In Honour of the 25th Anniversary of a Small Shul."

81 Richard Cohen. "Urban Visibility and the Biblical Vision-Jewish Culture in Western and Central Europe in the Modern Age."*Cultures of the Jews.* Edited by David Biale (Schocken Books, New York, 2002) p.748.

82 Ibid. p. 752 .

83 *Synagogues of Europe-Architecture, History, Meaning.* p.63.

84 Raphael Mahler. *Hasidism and the Jewish Enlightenment, Their*

Confrontation in Galicia and Poland in the First Half of the Nineteenth Century. Translated from Yiddish by Eugene Orenstein (Jewish Publication Society of America, Philadelphia, New York, Jerusalem 1985).

85 Ibid., quoted on p. 135.

86 Ibid., quoted on p.126.

87 Ibid. pp. 140-41.

88 Ibid., quoted on p. 148.

89 Alexander Guterman. "The Congregation of the Great Synagogue in Warsaw: Its Changing Social Composition and Ideological Affiliations." *Polin: Studies of Polish Jewry.* Edited by Antony Polansky. Volume II (Littman Library of Jewish Civilization, 1998) p.113.

90 Krzysztof Stefanski. "The Synagogues of Lodz." *Polin-Studies of Polish Jewry.* Edited by Antony Polansky. Volume II (Littman Library of Jewish Civilization, 1998) pp. 156-7.

91 The architecture of the rue Pavé synagogue is discussed in:

Jarrase. pp.147-8.

Krinsky, p.148.

92 Dominique Jarrase. p.148 quote of president of the congregation, J. Landau.

93 The Nusach Ha'ari was purchased by the Hasidic Belzer community in 2007. This community comprises many of the residents of the surrounding blocks. They have renovated the building again to suit their particular needs.

94 Krinsky. p.31.

95 Ibid. p.52.

96 I arrived at this estimate by concluding that the *aron hakodesh* would usually be on the wall opposite the entrance which faces the street. Therefore, only buildings on the east side of the street would result in a direction of prayer facing east.

97 Bill Surkis, taped interview.

98 Nathan Rosenoff, 50th anniversary speech, Allan Raymond collection, Archives of the JPL/Religion/Shevet Achim.

99 Walicki. p 79.

100 Ben Zion Dalfen, taped interview.

101 *Anshei Ozeroff*, Rabbi Yehoshua Halevi Herschorn, "In Honour of the 25th Anniversary of a Small Shul."

102 Israel Medres. *Tsvishn Tsvey Velt Milkhomes.* (Keneder Adler Press, Montreal, 1964) p.22. translated from the Yiddish by Sara Tauben

103 Lawrence Poliger, taped interview.

104 Krinsky, pp. 22, 49, 111.

105 Confirmed by Edward Caplansky in phone conversation April 19, 2004.

106 As quoted by Ira Robinson. *Rabbis and Their Community, Studies in the Eastern European Orthodox Rabbinate in Montreal, 1896-1930.* (University of Calgary Press, Calgary, 2007) p. 32.

107 M. Ginzburg. "Fifty Years of the Beth Congregation," pp. 78-80, translated by Sara Tauben. "The Beth David Congregation:Its Origin and History," 50th Anniversary publication, Outremont, Quebec, 1938. JPL Library Archive/synagogues/Beth David.

108 Ibid. author not noted, p. 9.

109 Ibid. R. Abramovitch, p. 13.

110 Ibid. Ginzburg.

111 Ibid. Louis H. Rohrlick, "The President's Message," pp 3-5

112 Ibid. "Beth David Congregation," Rabbi S. Herschorn, "Our Jubilee," pp12-13.

113 Ibid. R. Yehoshua Halevi Herschorn. "In Honour of the 25th Anniversary of a Small Shul."

114 Ibid.

115 The constitution of the synagogue is on the first page of the *pinkas*, the synagogue record book. Only a handful of entries follow the constitution. The book is in the hands of family members. The Hebrew word for "sons" can also be translated as "children" including both male and female. As the charter clearly includes Raizel's daughter, Haya Sara, as well as her four sons as the responsible heirs of the synagogue, I have used "children" instead of "sons" in the translation. Thanks to Professor Ira Robinson for his assistance in the translation of this poem.

116 David Kaufman. *Shul With a Pool.* (Brandeis University Press, University Press of New England, Hanover and London) p.2.

117 Adath Israel Anniversary publication, 1960.

118 David Rome, former archivist of the Canadian Jewish Congress Archives, David Rome synagogue file.

119 Congregation Anshei Ozeroff Silver Jubilee.

120 Rachel Wischnitzer. *The Architecture of the European Synagogue* (The Jewish Publication Society, Philadelphia, 1964) pp.xxx-xxxii and Samuel Gruber. *The American Synagogue* (Rizzoli, New York, 2003) pp.84-116.

121 Jarrassé. p.138.
122 Ibid.
123 Le Fondation du patrimoine religieux du Québec.

Glossary

adon olam
The closing song in the Sabbath morning prayer service in praise of "the Lord of the universe."

Aggadah
Part of the body of rabbinic interpretive literature that is comprised of ethical teachings, legends, tales and folklore.

aliyahs
(Hebrew: ascend) Ritual honours in a synagogue. The individual (men only in orthodoxy) is called up to the bimah or the Torah Ark to perform a ritual honour.

aron hakodesh
The Torah Ark which houses the Torah scrolls. Traditionally, it should be placed on the wall of the synagogue facing Jerusalem. In the West, this is the eastern wall.

bal koreh
A Torah reader, literally, a master of reading the Torah.

bal tefilah
A reader or chanter of prayers.

bar mitzvah
The coming of age ceremony for boys at age thirteen. It focuses on reading a portion of the Torah and Haftorah, a reading from the "Prophets" which corresponds to the weekly Torah portion.

battei midrash
Houses of study and worship.

beit din
Jewish court of law.

bimah
The reading table in a synagogue upon which the Toral scrolls are unrolled and read.

chanukos habais
(Yiddish and Hebrew) building dedication.

chanukat habeit
(Hebrew)

chazan	(Hebrew) Cantor. The member of the clergy who chants the prayers.
chazan sheini	Associate cantor.
cheder	(Hebrew: room)A religious school for young boys.
chevra kadisha	(Hebrew: the holy association) Burial society, traditionally an honorific and voluntary position.
cholent	(Yiddish) A slow cooked casserole made with beans, potatoes, vegetables, and, usually, beef.
chuppah	(Hebrew) The wedding canopy.
daven	(Yiddish) To worship.
drash	(Hebrew) An interpretation of Biblical text or law.
gabbai	In European traditional communities, an elected, unpaid communal leader responsible for various communal organizations. In a synagogue, he manages the affairs of the synagogue and is responsible for distributing ritual honours.
Gemara	See Talmud.
goyim	Non Jews.
Halachah	(Hebrew: walk or way) Jewish law comprised of "written law," that which is derived from Torah, and "oral law," according to tradition that which was received by Moses and passed on orally from generation to generation. It was eventually written as the Talmud and includes as well the entire authoritative rabbinic tradition. See Talmud and Torah.
Haredi	(Hebrew: tremble) A member of the ultra-orthodox community or the term designating the community itself.

Hasid	(Hebrew: a righteous person) The Hasidic movement, founded by Israel ben Eleazer, the Bal Shem Tov, in the late 18th century. The more accurate term to generally designate the ultra-orthodox community is Haredi.
Haskalah	(Hebrew: education) The Jewish Enlightenment
kehillah	(Hebrew: community)A traditional Jewish community in Eastern Europe at times having official government-sanctioned status.
keter	(Hebrew: crown) A silver Torah ornament.
kiddish	(Yiddish from the Hebrew *kiddush* meaning blessing) The ritual meal following services which require the blessing over wine and bread, but which is usually much more substantial.
kigels	(Yiddish) Casserole of noodles, potatoes, or other vegetables.
knaidlach	(Yiddish) Matzoh balls. Dumplings made from matzoh flour served in chicken soup.
Kohanim	Priests in the ancient Temple. Following the destruction of the Temple three lineages developed among Jews: Kohen, Levite, and Israelite. Kohanim and Levites, but particularly Kohanim, have ritual and religious obligations and privileges. Most Jews are Israelites.
kreplach	(Yiddish) Stuffed, usually boiled, dumplings, generally served in chicken soup.
landsleit	(Yiddish, or "landslayt") Countrymen.
landsmanshaft	(Yiddish) Mutual aid society for people from the same town.

latkes	(Yiddish) pancakes, generally potato pancakes.
lernen	(Yiddish) learning
luach	(Hebrew) calendar
maariv	See *shacharit*
magen david	(Hebrew: shield of David) Star of David. The six sided star was said to have marked David's shield.
maskilim	(Hebrew: educated) Followers of the Jewish Enlightenment.
mechitzah	(Hebrew: divider) A physical division between men and women in a synagogue.
midrash	(Hebrew: interpret) The body of rabbinic interpretive literature that refers to interpretations of biblical law. *Aggadah,* interpretive teachings, legends, and folklore are considered part of the *midrash*ic tradition.
mikveh	(Hebrew) Ritual bath.
minchah	See *shacharit*
minyan	(Hebrew, "minyanim" plural) A quorum of ten men (in traditional Judaism) required to conduct a communal prayer service.
Mishnah	See *Talmud*
mizrach	(Hebrew: eastern) In a synagogue it refers to the eastern wall or to a plaque or amulet attached to the eastern wall. The direction of prayer is prescribed as being towards Jerusalem. In the West, this means towards the East. The Torah ark is situated on the wall flanked by seats reserved for officers and other honourees. This prescribed orientation of synagogues is not consistently adhered to, but the wall housing the Torah ark is, never theless, referred to as the *mizrach* wall.

mitzvoth	(Hebrew: commandments) There are 613 commandments, obligations of observance.
mohel	(Hebrew, "mohelim" plural) Certified, ritual circumciser.
Nusah Sepharad	Sephardic ritual
Oneg Shabbath	(Hebrew: the enjoyment of Shabbath) A gathering that takes pleasure in Shabbath-readings, communal song, etc.
parochet	(Hebrew) Curtain covering the door which opens the Torah Ark.
parnas	(Hebrew: leader) An unpaid position sometimes synonymous with *gabbai*. In Europe, from the Middle Ages until the early modern period, the *parnas* was the leader of the community. In modern synagogues the president of a congregation is also the *parnas*.
rebbe	(Yiddish: rabbi) Generally refers to a Hasidic rabbi.
rebitzin	(Yiddish) A rabbi's wife.
responsas	Rabbinic responses to legal questions.
rimonim	(Hebrew: pomegranate or finial) Silver Torah ornaments which cover and decorate the handles used to unroll the scrolls.
Rosh Hashonah	Jewish New Year
schochet	(Hebrew)Ritual slaughterer of kosher meat.
Shabbes goy	A non-Jew, who performs services, usually for pay, for an observant Jew who does not wish to desecrate the Sabbath commandments.
shacharit, mincha, mariv	Morning, afternoon, and evening prayers.

shammash	A paid beadle or sexton in a community institution, synagogue, or court. He was sometimes responsible for calling the people to *shul*. The "*shulklaper,*" would knock on people's houses reminding them that services were about to begin. His role was also that of witnessing the signing of documents. He supervised the synagogue in a capacity that might be equivalent to today's executive director.
shtetle	(Yiddish)Eastern European Jewish village.
shtibel	(Yiddish "small room" or "small house") Small house of prayer, discussed in greater detail in the text.
shul	(Yiddish, derived from German; *shuln* plural) Synagogue. Also means school indicating the dual function of a synagogue as a house of worship, and a house of study. A *shulechel* is a small synagogue.
Shulchan Aruch	(Hebrew: an ordered table) Codification of Jewish law by Sephardi Rabbi Joseph Caro in the sixteenth century with commentary by Moses Isserles, an Ashkenasi rabbi.
simchah	(Hebrew and Yiddish with slight variance in pronounciation) A celebration.
Simhat Torah	The holiday celebrating the Torah which marks the last in the cycle of High Holidays in the fall.
succah	(Hebrew)A temporary structure built turning the eight days of the spring festival of *Succoth* All meals are to be taken in the *succah*.
tas	(Hebrew)A silver shield hung on the Torah which has a place for a removable plaque indicating the name of the Torah portion that will

be revealed when the Torah is unrolled.

talit   (Hebrew) Prayer shawl worn by men in synagogue. Women have also begun wearing *talitot* in liberal congregations.

Talmud   *Talmud* (from the Hebrew root meaning "teach") The Talmud is known as the oral law while the Torah is the written law. A complicated compendium of commentaries and discussions of Jewish law and practice, the Talmud combines two works known as Mishna and Gemara and is said to have been "closed" by the fifth century. However, the commentaries of Rashi (11th century) and his disciples were incorporated as sidebars and contemporary commentaries continue to be added to some additions.

Talmud Torah   Elementary level religious schools established by and subject to regulation by local Jewish communities in Europe. In Montreal the first Talmud Torah was initiated at the B'nai Jacob synagogue in 1886. The Talmud Torah of today, as other Jewish schools in Montreal, offers secular as well as religious studies and is recognized by the Quebec Ministry of Education.

Tanach   Torah plus 21 books of The Prophets *Nevi'im*) and the 13 books of The Writings (*Ketuvim*) comprise the Tanach (an acronym of the first letter of the three works), the Jewish Bible.

Torah   (Hebrew: teach)The Torah, as texts, contains the Five Books of Moses, the Pentateuch, which comprise the Written Law. But the concept of Torah also includes as well Oral Law which came to be composed as Talmud.

tzedakah   (Hebrew - "justice") Charity

Vad Ha'ir	The rabbinic council of Montreal.
yad	(Hebrew: "hand") A silver pointer used to point at and follow the reading of the Torah scroll.
yarmulke	(Yiddish; the Hebrew term is "kippa") Skullcap, head covering worn by men in synagogue and observant men, outside of synagogue.
yiddisher yid	(Yiddish: A Jewish Jew) An observant Jew.
yiskor	(Hebrew: remembrance) The annual commemoration of a death.
yom tov	(Hebrew: "good day") Holiday
yontif	(Yiddish) Holiday

SOURCES CONSULTED FOR GLOSSARY

Encyclopedia Judaica. Jerusalem: Keter Publishing House Ltd., Jerusalem, 1972.

Seltzer, Robert M. *Jewish People, Jewish Thought.* New Jersey: Prentice Hall, 1980.

Steinsalz, Rabbi Adin. *Steinsalz Edition of the Talmud.* New York: Random House, 1989.

Bibliography

ARCHIVES CONSULTED AND UNPUBLISHED MANUSCRIPTS

Canadian Jewish Congress Archives
    Series ZH (synagogue files)
    Synagogue files of David Rome
Jewish Public Library
    Religion files
Bibliotheque et Archives nationales du Québec
    City maps
Levitt, Sheldon, Milstone, Lyn, Tenenbaun, Sidney.
    "A Study of Canadian Synagogue Architecture:
    Synagogues of Quebec and the Maritime region." 1985
Rosenberg, Louis, head of the Bureau of Social and Economic
    Research, Canadian Jewish Congress, various demographic
    studies
Seidel, Judith. "The Development and Social Adjustment of the
    Jewish Community in Montreal." Masters thesis at
    McGill University, 1939
Other documents are cited in notes to the text.

ARCHIVAL MATERIAL IN PRIVATE HANDS
Various documents are cited in notes to the text.

SYNAGOGUE ARCHITECTURE AND JEWISH ART
Cohen, Richard. *Jewish Icons, Art and Society in Modern Europe.*
    Berkeley, Los Angeles, London: University of California
    Press, 1998.
Graham, Sharon. "An Examination of Toronto Synagogue Archi-
    tecture, 1897-1937." JSSAC/JSEAC 26, no. 3, 4(2001) pp.15-24
Gruber, Sam. *Synagogues.* New York: Michael Freedman Pub.
    Group, Inc.,1999.

Gruber, Sam. *American Synagogue: A Century of Architecture and Jewish Community.* New York: Rizzoli, 2003.

Gutmann, Joseph. *The Synagogue: Studies in Origins, Archeology, and Architecture.* New York: KTAV Publishing House Inc., 1975.

 Rosenau, Helen. "German Synagogues in the Early Period of Emancipation," pp. 317-333; Wischinitzer, Rachel. "The Egyptian Revival in Synagogue Architecture," pp. 334-350.

Gutmann, Joseph. *No Graven Images, Studies in Art and the Hebrew Bible.* New York: KTAV Publishing House, Inc., 1971.

 "Prolegomenon" pp. XI-LV

Israelowitz, Oscar. *Synagogues of the United States.* Brooklyn: Israelowitz Publishing, 1992.

Israelowitz, Oscar. *Synagogues of New York City.* New York: Dover Publications, Inc., 1982.

Jarrassé, Dominique. *Synagogues.* Paris: Société Nouvelle Adam Biro, 2001; English translation Paris: Vilo International, 2001

Krinsky, Carol Herselle. *Synagogues of Europe, Architecture, History, and Meaning.* New York: Architectural History Foundation, 1985.

Meek, H.A. *The Synagogue.* London: Phaidon Press Ltd., 1995.

Polonsky, Anthony. *Studies in Polish Jewry, vol. II (on religion).* Littman Library of Jewish Civilization, 1998.

 Bussang, Julian J. "The Progressive Synagogue in Lwow," pp. 127-153.

 Hubka, Thomas C. "Jewish Art and Architecture in the Eastern European Context: The Gwozdziec-Chodorow Group of Wooden Synagogues," pp. 141-182

 Gutterman, Alexander. "The Congregation of the Great Synagogue in Warsaw: Its Changing Social Composition and Ideological Affiliations," pp. 112-125.

Stephanski, Krzystof. "The Synagogues of Lodz," pp.154-167

Walicki, Jacek. *Synagogues and Prayer Houses of Lodz.* Translation by Guy Russel Torr. DRUK, Lodz, 2000

Wischnitzer, Rachel. *The Architecture of the European Synagogue.* Philadelphia: The Jewish Publication Society, 1964

Wolf, Gerald. *Synagogues of the Lower East Side of New York*

MATERIAL CULTURE

Golag, John. *The Architectural Interpretation of History.* New York: St. Martin's Press, 1975.

Waghorne, Joanne Punzo. *The Raja's Magic Clothes: Re-visioning Kingship and Divinity in England's India.* Philadelphia: University of Pennsylvania Press, 1994.

GENERAL AND MONTREAL JEWISH HISTORY

Biale, David, editor. *Cultures of the Jews: A New History.* New York: Schocken Books, 2002.

    Biale, David. "Preface: Towards a Cultural History of the Jews," pp.xvii-xxxiii.

    Cohen, Richard. "Urban Visibility and Biblical Visions: Jewish Culture in Western and Central Europe in the Modern Age," pp.731-796.

Figler, Bernard. *Canadian Jewish Profiles: Rabbi Dr. Herman Abramowitz, Lazarus Cohen, Lyon Cohen.* Ottawa: privately published, 1968.

Hart, Arthur Daniel, editor. *The Jew in Canada.* Montreal: Jewish Publications Ltd., 1926.

Kaufman, David. *Shul with a Pool, The Synagogue-Centre in American Jewish History.* Hanover and London: University Press of New England, 1999.

Jewish Year Book. London: Jewish Chronicle, first publication 1936.

Mahler, Raphael. *Hasidism and the Enlightenment: Their Confrontation in Galicia and Poland in the First Half of the Nineteenth Century.* Translated from the Yiddish by

Eugene Orenstein. Philadelphia, New York, Jerusalem: Jewish Publication Society of America, 1985

Medres, Israel. *Montreal Fun Nechten.* Montreal: The Eagle Publishing Co., Ltd., 1947

Medres, Israel. *Montreal of Yesterday: Jewish Life in Montreal 1900-1920.* Translated from the Yiddish by Vivian Felsen. Montreal: Véhicule Press, 2000

Medres, Israel. *Tvishen de Twvey Velt Milchomes.* Montreal: The Eagle Publishing Co., Ltd., 1964

Robinson, Ira, Anctil, Pierre and Butovsky, Mervin, eds. *An Everyday Miracle: Yiddish Culture in Montreal. Montreal:* Véhicule Press 1990.

Wolofsky, Hirsch. *Journey of My Life.* Montreal: The Eagle Publishing Co., Ltd., 1945

ASTROLOGY IN JUDAISM

Glazerman, Matityhu. *Above the Zodiac: Astrology in Jewish Thought.* Nothvale, New Jersey: Jason Aronson, Inc., 1997.

Langerman, Zvi. "Some Astrological Themes in the Thought of Abraham Ibn Ezra," *Rabbi Ibn Ezr; Studies in the Writings of a Twelfth Century Polymath.* Edited by Isadore Twersky and Jay M. Harris. Cambridge: Harvard University Press, 1993, pp. 28-85.

Sirat, Colette. "The Neo-Platonists: Astrology and Israel," *A History of Jewish Philosophy of the Middle Ages.* Cambridge, England: Cambridge University Press. 1995, pp.57-93.

In the Footsteps of the Past

NORTHERN TOUR:

10. **Beth Hakneseth Anshei Ukraina**
    5116, rue Saint-Urbain

11. **B'nai Jacob**
    172, avenue Fairmont Ouest

12. **Zerei Dath V'Doath**
    5457, rue Jeanne-Mance

13. **Nusach Ha'ari / Avath Shalom**
    5583, rue Jeanne-Mance

14. **Tifereth Israel**
    5390, rue Saint-Urbain

15. **Anshei Ozeroff**
    5244, rue Saint Urbain

16. **Chevra Kadisha**
    5213, rue Hutchinson

17. **Beth David**
    422, boulevard Saint-Joseph O.

18. **Yavna B'nai Parnass Shul**
    4690, rue Hutchinson

SOUTHERN TOUR:

1. **Shaare Tefilah**
   29, rue Milton Ouest

2. **Shomrim Laboker**
   3675, rue Saint-Dominique

3. **Nusach Ha'ari**
   100, avenue des Pins Est

4. **Beth Yehuda**
   214, rue Duluth Est

5. **Pinsker Shul**
   4259, rue de Bullion

6. **Kerem Israel**
   4335, rue Saint-Dominique

7. **Beth Hamedrash Chevra Shaas**
   4170, rue Saint Urbain

8. **Stepener Shul**
   4115, rue Saint-Urbain

9. **Temple Solomon (Bagg Street Shul)**
   3919, rue Clark

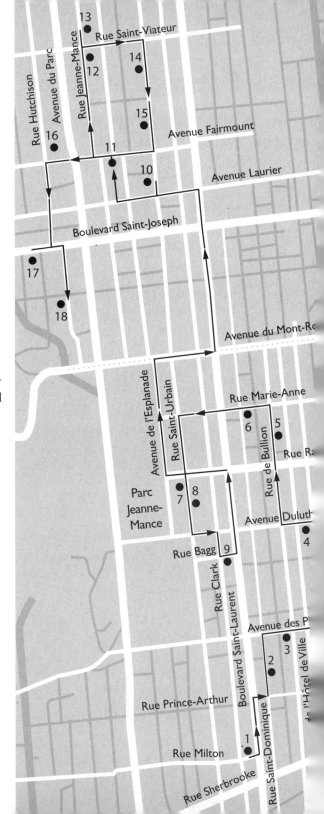

WALKING TOUR

In the Footsteps of the Past

~

Discovering Montreal's
Early Synagogues

In the Footsteps of the Past is designed to help the tourist and Montreal resident alike discover traces of Montreal's Jewish heritage in a dynamic contemporary neighbourhood. While the primary objective is to locate the remnants of historic synagogues, visitors are encouraged to enjoy the Plateau Mont-Royal of today. Note its fashionable boutiques, trendy restaurants, ethnic eateries, typical rowhouses, and the charm of its alleyways.

Don't expect to encounter landmarks of monumental significance. Instead, you will discover hidden gems covered over by various stages of urban layering. Each one, however, will reveal an aspect of the lives, values, and aspirations of an immigrant community.

Useful Information

The tour is divided into a southern and a northern section which can be followed independently or contiguously. Each section can be completed in about two hours on foot or by a one hour bike tour. Sunday is the best day for biking, when the narrow streets are less congested. The route has been created to direct the biker in the correct direction on the many one-way streets. Pedestrians can feel free to diverge. Alternatively, biking and walking could be combined using Bixi, Montreal's unique bike rental system. There are many Bixi rental stations in this area (www.bixi.com).

Visitors please note that on street signs "est" means "east" and "ouest" means "west."

Tour A: The Southern Section

Now let us *shpatzir* or stroll through "Montreal of Yesterday," as author and journalist Israel Medres invited us to do in his book of the same name. Of the once thriving and congested Jewish neighbourhood that he described in the oldest parts of the city, little was evident even in 1947 when he wrote his book. Therefore we begin our journey slightly further north on the corner of boulevard Saint-Laurent and rue Sherbrooke, a significant intersection both in the development of Montreal and the history of the Jewish community.

Useful Information
Boulevard Saint-Laurent and rue Sherbrooke

Starting point: corner of boulevard Saint-Laurent and rue Sherbrooke.

Getting there: Sherbrooke bus 24 or bus 55 north from Saint-Laurent Métro.

Prior arrangements: **The Bagg Street Shul** is the only pre-war synagogue in the area still functioning. With prior planning, Michael Kaplan will be happy to welcome you. He can be contacted by email at baggshul@gmail.com or directly at 514-791-8344.

When you get hungry: There is no shortage of restaurants in the area known as Plateau-Mont-Royal. Unfortunately, there are no kosher restaurants, but there are three Jewish landmark eateries nearby. **Moishe's Steakhouse** at **3961 Saint-Laurent**, at the corner of Bagg, is particularly famous for their steaks but has a full menu including many Ashkenazi favourites. **Schwartz's Hebrew Delicatessen, 3895 Saint-Laurent**, is Montreal's legendary smoked meat destination. **Wilensky's Light Lunch** at **34 rue Fairmont ouest**, corner Clark, largely unchanged since its establishment in the thirties was featured in the movie *The Apprenticeship of Duddy Kravitz*. The well-established vegetarian restaurant, **Café Santropol** at **3990 Saint-Urbain** on the corner of Duluth, is worth mentioning not only for its healthy and moderately-priced menu, but also for its environmentally-conscious meals-on-wheels charity including rooftop gardening and a bike maintenance program.

Boulevard Saint-Laurent appears on city maps as early as 1672. Bearing the same name as the river from which it emanates, it formed the city's first north-south road carrying produce and goods between farm settlements and the harbour. As the city grew, it came to be known as "The Main," the primary artery of urban development and industrialization. Called boulevard Saint-Laurent in French and St. Lawrence Boulevard in English, it divides the traditionally French eastern from the English western parts of the city. It has served as the immigrant corridor, the multicultural portal that is still evident today.

Rue Sherbrooke developed as the city's first major east-west artery. The city expanded westward with the establishment of "The Golden Square Mile," the geographic core of Montreal's early 20th century economic and commercial development as well as prominent residences. This area is encompassed in today's *centreville* or downtown. Further west, the original country estates built to take advantage of the pleasant nature and summer climate of the "foothills" of Montreal's Mount Royal, came to be the prominent residential municipality of Westmount. Sherbrooke also marks a threshold as the Eastern European Jewish immigrants began to leave their first area of settlement in the oldest parts of the city, known today as Old Montreal and Chinatown. (See Chapter I, "Harbingers of Great Institutions–Uptown and Downtown" for a history of Montreal's earliest Jewish communities.)

▶ Begin your journey on the north-west corner of rue Sherbooke and boulevard Saint-Laurent in front of the gas station. Walk north to rue Milton just behind the station. The **Shaare Tefilah** [1] once existed on the corner of Milton and Clark.

The Shaare Tefilah Synagogue, circa 1925.

Erected in the first decade of the twentieth century, the impressive structure was the first synagogue built above Sherbrooke. When the congregation moved to a post-war neighbourhood in the late 1950s, the building was converted to the Elysée Theatre which was razed in the late 1980s to make way for the present building housing Softimage, the company that created the 3-D effects for movies such as *Harry Potter* and *Lord of the Rings*, and Ex-Centris, a state-of- the art- film production and screening facility, as well as ground-floor boutiques and restaurants.

East of boulevard Saint-Laurent

Continue north one block on the east side of Saint-Laurent and turning right at rue Prince-Arthur, a lively pedestrian mall lined with restaurants, café's, artisan shops, and featuring street performers on summer evenings. Turn left at **rue Saint-Dominique** to 3675, the former **Shomrim Laboker [2]**. The original deed of sale dates the purchase of this property to 1913. The signatures on the deed attest to the working-class status of this and most of the other congregations in this immigrant area: "Ephraim Rosenblatt, butcher, Max Lichterman, tailor,

C. Drucker, presser, Aaron Previn, merchant." Shulamis Yelin, a well-known teacher, poet, and author, recalled the festive opening of the synagogue on Simchat Torah in 1918. The children, dressed in their finest, marched to *shul* carrying flags emblazoned with figures of the Lion of Judah. Her own excitement was heightened as her grandfather, a skilled carpenter, had carved the *aron hakodesh* and her mother and aunt had sewn and decorated the Torah covers.* The participation of the members in creating components of their synagogue demonstrated a prevalent commitment to the creation and beautification of these *shuln*.

While a few of the synagogues were purpose-built and architecturally significant, most accommodated themselves within existing residential or commercial units. This building was converted and enlarged from a duplex. A women's gallery, created on the second floor, was illustrated with signs of the zodiac and illuminated by double rows of stained glass windows. A telltale section of a cornice moulding, partially

*Shulamis Yelin. *Shulamis: Stories from a Montreal Childhood* (Shoreline, 1993) pp. 28-30.

embedded in the brick, marks the point at which the vestibule lobby was extended from the original building. Note the same moulding still evident on the buildings to the right. The brickwork on the façade features a mysterious element: The symbol most commonly used to designate a synagogue, the Star of David, is depicted sideways instead of pointing up. This may have been a quirk of a particular mason as the same detail can be seen on a synagogue further north whose bricks date to the same decade.

▶Continue walking north on Saint-Dominique, turning right on avenue des Pins. Merely a block away, at the corner of avenue Coloniale, an imposing new modern structure, Théâtre Quat' Sous, marks the location of the earlier **Nusach Ha'ari** [3]. For many years the theatre operated out of the former synagogue which had itself been converted

The building that once housed the Nusach H'ari synagogue was demolished in August, 2007.

from a building housing four or five residential units.

▶Proceed east two blocks to Hôtel-de-Ville. Cross the street and begin walking north on Hotel-de-Ville, through what is now predominantly a Portuguese neighbourhood. After you have crossed rue Roy, look up the street. On the right side, the street is dominated by a brick building with a peaked roof. On the rear elevation a faint delineation in the brick work recalls what was once a large circular window with a Star of David, illuminating the space above the *aron hakodesh*. A discerning eye can spot such traces of the past on many buildings once used as synagogues. Keep your eyes open for other such markings during the tour. Bikers should continue onto the next block, avenue Laval, north to avenue Duluth.

While tucked into a side street, the **Beth Yehuda** [4], **214 Duluth est**, was, nevertheless, an imposing structure in contrast to the surrounding two-storey residential buildings. A newspaper article announcing the opening in 1923 proclaimed it to be "one of the most beautiful synagogues in Canada." However, the elaborate building presented a financial challenge for decades to come. The synagogue was nearly forfeited to the bank shortly after opening. Six years later, not only did the stock market crash deal a financial blow, but the wealthier residents were already moving out of the area, leaving the synagogue "a widow" with deficits, debts, and expenses. The congregation's aspirations to acquire a fine building clearly exceeded affordability. The building underwent a rather awkward conversion into apartments in the 1960s. Whatever remains of the architectural elements of the synagogue can only be viewed from a distance.

Our tour continues two blocks west and north on rue de Bullion. However, you might decide to linger awhile on Duluth. Lined with moderately-priced restaurants of all kinds, Duluth is a favourite for locals and visitors alike.

▶ Walk one block west from the former Beth Yehuda to de Bullion and continue north until you reach **4259 rue de Bullion**. This building , once the **Pinsker Shul [5]**, has been reconverted to a residential dwelling with an apartment on each floor. The doorway has a metal canopy probably built by the synagogue. A Star of David, now replaced by a cross,

probably once topped the canopy. The presence of the cross is curious since the building never served a Christian religious function.

The Pinsker Shul is an example of a *landsmanshaft shul* typical of most of the smaller immigrant congregations. The *landsmanshaft* was a mutual aid society established by immigrants from the same area or town. When the term was applied to a synagogue, it indicated that members likely shared friendships and familial connections in the Old Country and provided each other with a measure of assistance and support in their adopted city. The members of this congregation originated from Pinsk, Russia. While the exterior of the building was likely as modest as it appears today, the interior featured ornamental woodwork, wall illustrations, and a star-studded ceiling. But, as befitted a place where everyone knew each other, "the decorum was lively and noisy."

▶ Follow de Bullion, turning left on rue Marie-Anne to Parc du Portugal honouring Montreal's Portuguese community at Saint-Dominique. A plaque reads: "We arrived in this area seeking a new life and ample horizons." The park's gazebo provides a pleasant place to rest as well as a good view of **4335 Saint-Dominique**. The simple two-storey rectangular building holds no clue as to its former vocation as a synagogue. But a simple sketch by architect Harry Stillman takes us back to the early part of the 20th century. Behind the groups of people milling about and lounging on the park's benches the synagogue is depicted, punctuated by a small arched parapet on the roofline.

The **Kerem Israel [6]** was a family-owned synagogue founded in 1910 by Pinchas Parnass. The second floor served not as a women's gallery but as a free school for children. In 1926, following the movement of the community further north and west, Pinchas bought another synagogue in honour of his wife, Raizel. Kerem Israel continued to function until sometime in the 1960s while the newer Yavna B'nai Parnass Shul served its surrounding community until the late nineties.

West of boulevard Saint-Laurent

Our route continues west along Marie-Anne, crossing boulevard Saint-Laurent, until you reach rue Saint-Urbain. Turn left. On route to the next former synagogue, you will pass an important landmark in Montreal Jewish history. The building at **4251 rue Saint-Urbain** once housed **Baron Byng High School**. The school graduated many illustrious individuals, the most famous, perhaps, being the author Mordecai Richler, who grew up on the street and wrote about it in his novels. Having already passed several synagogue buildings in but a few blocks, you can begin to appreciate that this was once a densely-populated Jewish area. Jewish students comprised a majority in the local public

Kerem Israel can be seen, on the right, in Harry Stillman's drawing.

schools. Yet the schools they attended were Protestant. At the time, Quebec public schools were either Protestant or Catholic. Jewish students, since 1903, were delegated to the Protestant system. In response, the community eventually established a vibrant and diverse network of Jewish private schools. In the 1990s the "confessional" system was replaced with separate English and French school boards. But now we are broaching on the complex, but not uninteresting, subject of Québec linguistic politics. In the 1990s the school building was purchased by Sun Youth, a charitable organization founded in 1954 to serve the recreational needs of the neighbourhood's youth. Today Sun Youth provides services to youth and seniors, operates a vital food bank and is often the first responder in times of critical needs and emergencies.

On your left, at **4081 Saint-Urbain,** you will see the old location for **Paperman & Sons,** a funeral home that has served the Jewish community for over ninety years.

The corner of rue Rachel and rue Saint-Urbain defines a significant place in today's Portuguese community. A large church is located on the south-east corner and a community centre stands across the street at **4170 rue Saint-Urbain.** The words inscribed in a recessed circle above the entrance identify the building as the Association Portuguese. But a Hebrew inscription just below the circle is still visible. **Beth Hamedrash Chevra Shaas** [7] was one of the larger synagogues and more veteran congregations in the area. This building is the first of many that we will encounter that were sold to subsequent groups of immigrants for use as community centres or places of worship.

Just to the south and across the street, the cottage at **4115 rue Saint-Urbain** once housed the **Stepener Shul** (8) and previously, one of the earlier locations of the Jewish Public Library.

▶ Following rue Saint-Urbain south, turn left on avenue Duluth and right on rue Clark. The corner of rue Clark and rue Bagg features the only still-functioning synagogue in the area and one of the two oldest synagogue buildings in Montreal. Of all the tiny gems you will have uncovered in this tour, this is the jewel in the crown: **Temple Solomon, Bagg Street Shul** [9], **3919 rue Clark.** If you have made previous arrangements, Michael Kaplan will greet you at the door of the Bagg Street Shul. And while he is pleased to welcome visitors, he is even happier to receive those who come to participate, to *daven*, to join them during services. "Best of all," he emphasizes, "everything at Bagg Street is free of charge, including High Holiday seats. Membership is acquired by coming on a *shabbos*, choosing a seat, and *shabbos* after *shabbos*, keeping that seat warm."

It is generally acknowledged that this building, converted from a duplex in 1921, is the longest lasting unaltered synagogue in Montreal. While the style of the building does not immediately communicate its purpose, the multiple Stars of David identify it as a synagogue. The cornerstone plaque indicates that the congregation is composed of *anshei sepharad*—people of Spain. Ethnically, the congregation was Ashkenazi, probably Russian. The use of the Sephardic ritual was, however, not uncommon in some of the smaller synagogues, a practice influenced by Hasidic custom in Eastern Europe.

The interior layout remains an example of a typical small urban synagogue. The tiny vestibule contains the stairway leading to the women's gallery. The main sanctuary is divided into the traditional main level reserved for men. Above, the U-shaped balcony serves as the women's gallery. Much of the woodwork, including the *aron hakodesh* originating from Belgium, was acquired from the Shaar Hashomayim when it moved from its McGill Street location in downtown Montreal to Westmount in 1922. These artifacts remain as reminders of the original distinctions between the established and the immigrant communities and continue to symbolically connect Montreal's two oldest synagogues. (See discussion on the "uptown-downtown" communities in Chapter 1).

The illustrations on the balustrade of the women's section, representing the zodiac, provide a link between Jewish folk expression of Eastern Europe and Canada. The signs of the zodiac formed an important part of the Eastern European folk art iconography, astrology being an ancient element within Judaism. Illustrations of the zodiac, often enmeshed in intricate floral designs, depictions of animals, and lines of Biblical texts decorated the interiors of Eastern European synagogues, most notably, the walls and ceilings of the wooden synagogues of Russia and Poland. These wooden synagogues were almost certainly built and designed by Christians but the existence, even names, of Jewish mural painters is well documented.* The small Bagg Street Shul still retains the simple, folk-art illustrations of the zodiac drawn by a father and son named Shadewasser.

The paintings are lent a certain Canadian character with the depictions of the bison, moose, and reindeer.

Virgo, *bitulah, Elul.*

The exterior of the building recently underwent a renovation under a grant provided by the provincial government for restoration of religious properties. Temple Solomon was the first synagogue in Montreal to receive such funding. Later, the basement was renovated and equipped with a modern kitchen making this a wonderful venue for small bar mitzvahs, weddings, or anniversaries.

▶Looking south, across the street you will notice a rather awkward tower-like protrusion on the façade of **3880 rue Clark**. A small congregation once worshipped on the ground floor of the home of Itzchak Lutterman. As the membership grew, the Lutterman family moved out, and the second floor was converted into a women's gallery accessed by a new exterior stairway enclosed in the tower. The congregation named itself **Beth Itzchak** in honor of Mr. Luttterman.

▶Further afield on rue Clark is a synagogue that no longer can be seen. **4299 rue Clark** was the location of **Chevra Thilim Linath Hatzedek**, a small one-storey building, hardly remarkable even then. But the Jewish value embedded in the name is worth noticing. *Chevra Thilim,* The Brotherhood of the Psalms, indicates that Psalms were recited every morning. *Linath Hatzedek* (A Night of Justice), refers to the *mitzvah* of sitting vigil through the night at the bedside of an ailing person, a commandment explicitly

*Thomas Hubka, "The Gwozdziec-Chodorow Group of Wooden Synagogues." *"Polin"* vol. II, ed. Anthony Polansky (Littman Library of Jewish Civilization, 1998) pp141-182.
**According to Joe Brick, caretaker of the synagogue.

indicated in the constitution of this *shul.*

Connecting Tour

The inter-war years marked a period of intensive settlement in the area north of avenue du Mont-Royal centred on avenue du Parc. Not only synagogues, but also many institutions defined the Jewish character of this area serving all age groups, a variety of political orientations and educational ideologies.

▶From the **Bagg Street Shul**, turn right on Bagg and continue the tour north on boulevard Saint-Laurent. You will pass Beacon Luminaire Inc. at **4075 Saint-Laurent.** This building housed the editorial offices and the typesetting and printing facilities of Montreal's Yiddish daily, the *Keneder Adler* (*The Eagle*) which was founded in 1907. Notice the shield-shaped emblems above the windows which symbolize the diversity of Montreal's citizens. (From left to right: maple leaves, fleur-de-lys, rose, thistle, harp, and the Star of David partly hidden under the For Rent sign).

▶Turn left at rue Rachel, and right at avenue de l'Esplanade, passing Parc Jeanne-Mance, better known to the Jewish community as Fletcher's Field.

Two buildings recalling previous Jewish institutions can be seen when you reach Mont-Royal. To your left, the elegant building between rue Jeanne-Mance and avenue du Parc, recently converted to condos, was built as the Young Men's and Young Women's Hebrew Association in 1929. The striking modern building at 120 Mont-Royal ouest was built in 1953 by the Jewish Public Library. Unfortunately, by the mid-fifties the community was already moving out of the area. Both institutions are now located in the Jewish community campus built in the 1970s in the Snowdon area at Côte Sainte-Catherine and Westbury.

▶To continue to Tour B: The Northern Section, turn right on avenue du Mont-Royal. Pedestrians should turn left on rue Saint-Urbain and bikers continue left on boulevard Saint-Laurent. Turn left at avenue Laurier.

The former YM-YWHA building on Mont-Royal.

Tour B: The Northern Section

Avenue Laurier and rue Saint-Urbain

Starting point: corner of avenue Laurier and rue Saint-Urbain
Getting there: Laurier Métro, then bus 51, or bus 55
When you get hungry: Montreal's famous original bagel
bakeries are located in this area. The bagels are best enjoyed
right out of the wood-burning ovens: **Fairmont Bagel, 74
avenue Fairmont ouest** and **Saint Viateur Bagel, 263 avenue
Saint-Viateur ouest.** Cheskies, around the corner at **359 rue
Bernard ouest** is a modern kosher bakery. Avenue du Parc is
lined with many excellent Greek fish restaurants. Check the
menus as prices vary from moderate to outrageously
expensive. Rue Laurier ouest (from boulevard Saint-Laurent
to Côte Sainte-Catherine) is now a fashionable street with a
variety of excellent restaurants at all price points, and was
once home to a bustling Jewish community including the
author's husband and maternal grandparents.

East of avenue du Parc

The building at **5116 Saint Urbain,**
now the Ukrainian Evangelical
Pentecostal Church, still bears
many markings of the **Beth
Haknesseth Anshei Ukraina[10].**
Some of the Hebrew letters,
indicating the name of the
congregation, engraved in
a stone above the doorway,
are still visible. Cornerstone
plaques, dating the building
to 1940, recognize not only
the officers but, unique to this
building, acknowledge the
contributions of the Ladies
Auxiliary. "They too
volunteered and contributed to
the construction of this
building." Look up at the metal
plaque with the symbol of the
cross. The stained-glass window
with the Star of David is still
visible from inside the building.
If you pass by on a Sunday
afternoon following church
services, you may have the good
luck of being able to go inside.

The interior of the former synagogue is stripped of any original decoration except for the murals which cover the balustrade of the former women's gallery. The paintings depict buildings, biblical or holy land sites, of which two, Rachel's Tomb and the Western Wall, are easily recognizable and are clearly of Jewish origin. The others have yet to be identified. The minister of the church confirmed that the paintings were created by the synagogue and that, as the church too accepts the teachings of the Old Testament, the murals were conserved.

▶Return to Laurier and follow it west, turning right into the alley just past avenue du l'Esplanade. At the end on your right, a prominent barrel-vaulted building with a circular tracing in the brick, formerly housing a stained-glass Star of David, provides the first hint that the building was once a synagogue. The **B'nai Jacob** [11], established in 1886, is one of the oldest of the Eastern European congregations. Originally located in a synagogue built by the Shaar Hashomayim in Old Montreal, B'nai Jacob continued to fill a prominent role in the community as the first synagogue built north of avenue du Mont-

Royal. This was the largest and most elaborate of the immigrant synagogues. The building now houses the Collège Français, **185 Fairmount ouest**. Its interior has been entirely gutted and the façade obliterated by a modernist extension on top of which the Hebrew inscription in the arch remains partially visible: "Through these portals the righteous will enter."

The former B'nai Jacob in today's cityscape.

▶ Continue west on avenue Fairmont turning right on rue Jeanne-Mance. Moving along this street, you might notice that many of the residents are Hasidic. The Hasidic communities, quite evident today on the streets east and west of avenue du Parc and into the adjacent municipality of Outremont, were largely established after World War II and have remained in the area. All of today's synagogues, mostly tucked away in residential buildings, belong to various Hasidic sects. A brown aluminum arch over the door of **5336 Jeanne-Mance** marks the entrance of the Belzer Shul. Follow the glow of florescent strip lights in the buildings to the left as an indication of the number of row-houses that were integrated as the spatial needs of the congregation grew.

The small triplex at the corner of Saint-Viateur at **5457 Jeanne-Mance** once housed the small *shtibel* of congregation **Zerei Dath V'Doath** [12]. Though not actually a Hasidic congregation, it was modelled after the Hasidic *beiti midrash* of Europe, small houses of prayer, with a focus on traditional study of Torah and Talmud.

As you pass the corner it is worth taking a glance east along Saint-Viateur. The magnificent Saint Michael's Church comes into view and serves as a strik-ing contrast in scale not only to the *shtibel* but even to the prominent **B'nai Jacob**.

▶ Cross the street to **5583 Jeanne-Mance**. An immigrant congregation worshiped in this location from the mid-thirties, converting a two-story duplex into a synagogue in 1947. For many years, the congregation

Nusach Ha'ari/Ahavath Sholem [13] had been able to maintain the building through the sale of well-located cemetery plots purchased decades ago that are now in high demand. Following the death of the long-time caretaker and as a result of a dwindling membership, the building was sold to the Belzer Hasidim in 2007. Walk back to rue Saint-Viateur turning left, or east and then right on **rue Saint-Urbain** to **5390**. It is hard to imagine that the Mediterranean-style building with terracotta-tiled roof was once an Eastern European

The Ten Commandments tablets and the menorah grillwork were still evident when Tifereth Israel became a Baptist church.

synagogue. Archival photos reveal that markings of the synagogue, **Tifereth Israel** [14], did survive the earlier incarnations by Baptist and Greek churches with a final act of urban layering creating a complete transformation into the Greek church of today. If you can make your way to the rear of the building, you will see the trace of the circular window, a feature identifying many of the former synagogues.

▶Continue south to **5244 Saint-Urbain**. This congregation occupied four or five commercial and residential locations before converting this duplex in 1943. The conversion of existing buildings was not only more economical than the construction of new ones but was, as well, a practical means of accommodating a membership that continued to move with considerable frequency. Such small *shuln* were not just houses of worship but also significant gathering places for *landsleit,* people from the same town. The **Anshei Ozeroff**[15] (the people of Ozeroff), immigrated from a small town in central Poland and remained committed to staying together in their new city.

West of avenue du Parc

Turning right on Fairmont, you will be able to have another look at the former B'nai Jacob before crossing avenue du Parc. The next three buildings you will see were originally built as churches. In 1925, the Methodist Church, Congregational Union, and Presbyterian Church amalgamated to form the United Church of Canada. They sold their individual churches at a time when the more affluent families of the Jewish immigrant community began to take up residence in the pleasant tree-lined streets of Outremont.

▶ Stop at the corner of rue Hutchinson. The **Chevra Kadisha** [16], **5213 Hutchison**, was the first of the immigrant

Today's Ukrainian Federation building on Hutchison was once the Chevra Kadisha synagogue.

congregations to build its own synagogue in 1903 in Old Montreal. Unfortunately, it was destroyed by fire in 1920. The building before you, a former Methodist church, was

163

purchased in 1927. The building underwent considerable interior and exterior renovation in its conversion to a Jewish house of worship, including raising the roof and adding a second floor to accommodate the women's gallery and creating arched parapets on the façade and side. The arch is an important architectural element associated with synagogues. Today's Ukrainian Federation has a straight roofline.

▶ Continue south on Hutchison two blocks to boulevard Saint-Joseph. Just to your right is an imposing Russian Orthodox church. Originally built as the Saint Giles Presbyterian Church, it was purchased by the **Beth David** [17], the Rumanian *shul,* in 1929.

Saint Giles Presbyterian Church, before it became the Beth David Rumanian *shul* in 1929.

It was the last of the older congregations to move out of the earliest area of settlement. It positioned itself as a religious, educational, and social centre.

The spacious sanctuary and well-equipped reception facilities made this synagogue the choice for many formal weddings. Only at the Beth David could the bridal procession be accompanied by the deep tones of the organ inherited from the church. Such practices drew considerable disapproval from more traditional elements of the community.

▶ Cross Saint-Joseph and continue down Hutchison towards our last destination. Just before you get there, it's worth noting that A.M. Klein, considered one of Canada's greatest poets, and whose writing reflected Jewish values, once lived at **4857.**

The former **Yavna B'nai Parnass Shul** [18], **4690 Hutchison** was dedicated to serving the surrounding community. In 1926 the Seventh Day Adventist congregation wished to sell this small red-brick church to a community who observed the Sabbath. The Parnass family took advantage of the opportunity to establish their second family *shul.* Today, although it is a private residence, the markings of the synagogue are obvious. The Tablets of the Ten Commandments top an inscription honouring and memorializing the founders, Pinchas and Raizel Parnass. The word "Yavna" is inscribed in the Stars of David. Yavna, an important centre of rabbinic study in ancient Palestine, served as a symbol of the family's ongoing dedication to Jewish education. As in their earlier synagogue, Kerem Israel (see the southern tour), the second floor was reserved as a free school for children.

We hope that your journey has been rewarded with unexpected discoveries as you followed in the footsteps of the Montreal Jewish community of yesterday.

Image Credits

2 courtesy of Eiran Harris; 19-20 Map drawn by Dave Goulet; 22 (top) 150th anniversary publication, CJCA; 22 (bottom) Jewish Times, December, 1899; 25 Charles E. Goad map 1879, Bibliothèque nationale du Québec; 26 150th anniversary publication, CJCA; 28 courtesy of photographer Emilio Guerra; 29 (top) Orthodox synagogue, postcard, circa 1910; 29 (bottom) Reform synagogue, copyright unknown; 30 Notman Photographic Archives, McCord Museum; 32 National Monuments Service, Budapest; 34 (top) Notman Photographic Archives, McCord Museum; 34 (bottom) Congregation Shaar Hashomayim; 37 Notman Photographic Archives, McCord Museum; 47 Notman Photographic Archives, McCord Museum; 51 Arial Subar, *Hazzanut in Montreal.* Council of Hazzanim of Greater Montreal, 1971, p. 46; 53 (top) Archives of Chevra Kadisha B'nai Jacob, *Photo Illustrations of Canada*; 53 (bottom) Witschnitzer, *The Architecture of European Synagogues*, p. 211; 54 Archives of Chevra Kadisha B'nai Jacob, *Photo Illustrations of Canada*; 57-58 by author; 61 (top) 50th anniversary publication, courtesy of Eiran Harris; 61 (bottom) by author; 68 courtesy Jean Zwirek and Rachel Birnbaum; 71 courtesy Jean Zwirek and Rachel Birnbaum; 76 (top) by author; 76 (bottom) courtesy Jean Zwirek and Rachel Birnbaum; 78 Archives of Tiffereth Beth David Jerusalem; 80 (top and bottom) by author; 82 by author; 83 (top and middle) courtesy of Helen Constantine; 83 (bottom) courtesy of Harry Stillman; 84 photo by Sid Tenenbaum, Ontario Jewish Archives, fonds 64, series 1, file 33; 87 (top) by author; 87 (bottom) drawn by Andre Engel; 89 by author; 95 (top) *Montreal Daily Witness*; 95 (bottom) 50th anniversary publication, 1938, Jewish Public Library Archives; 96 (top) postcard; 96 (bottom) Archives of Chevra Kadisha-B'nai Jacob; 101 Jewish Public Library Archives; 103 courtesy of Helen Constantine; 108 Canadian Jewish Congress Archives; 111-12 Canadian Jewish Congress Archives; 114 (top) Archives, Adath Israel; 114 (bottom) 25th Silver Jubilee, 1965, Jewish Public Library Archives; 119 letterhead of Hadrath Kodesh, Jewish Public Library Archives; 122 by author; 124 by author; 151; 153 by Simon Dardick; 155 courtesy Harry Stillman; 158 by author; 159-by Simon Dardick; 163 by author. 164 25th Silver Jubilee, 1965, Jewish Public Library Archives.

Index

Véhicule Press
www.vehiculepress.com